STUDIES IN MODERN EUROPEAN LITERATURE
AND THOUGHT

General Editor:
E R I C H H E L L E R
Professor of German
in the University College of Swansea

B A U D E L A I R E

BAUDELAIRE

BY

P. MANSELL JONES

NEW HAVEN

YALE UNIVERSITY PRESS

1952

TO

MADAME N. KHALIL BEY

I

'Baudelaire est au comble de la gloire,' said Paul Valéry twenty-five years ago, claiming that the small volume of *Les Fleurs du Mal* balanced in the esteem of literary connoisseurs the most illustrious and most spacious of *œuvres*. Its translation into the majority of European languages was a fact which seemed to him without parallel in the history of French literature. There can have been no more complete reversal of judgment on a modern poet than this *volte-face* from the bourgeois condemnation of 1857 for an offence against morals, resulting in a costly *succès de scandale*, to the elevation of the victim to the position he now occupies at the apex of French poetry in the nineteenth century. For whom in that field need Baudelaire fear? Hugo or Rimbaud? Mallarmé or Valéry? Over the distillers of quintessence Baudelaire has the advantage of being as comprehensible as a classic. One after another his works are in fact coming to figure among our classics as the decades add to our knowledge of their worth. Rimbaud alone challenges, if he does not surpass, Baudelaire in intensity. So far however an uncompromising originality of form has kept the work of 'Shakespeare enfant' from that breadth of attention for which the legend of his meteoric career appears to have prepared the way. As for Hugo, so steeply has his domination declined since the days when he could without too much presumption auscultate his heart for the sonorous echo of the universe, that Gide's recent temporizing over his notorious verdict, 'Hugo, hélas!' is not likely to end the partial eclipse by a mere stroke of the pen. Hugo remains in the penumbra, a 'phenomenon', in Thibaudet's word, someone very different from 'Victor in drama, Victor in romance', still for most of us unidentified. Baudelaire has variety but little of Hugo's virtuosity. His poetry, for many of his contemporaries, suffered by comparison with the quasi-epic pictorialism of his gigantic elder. Yet if his imaginative powers have not the range of Hugo's visual gift, they can approach at times the terrible perspicacity of Racine and reveal the depth and tumult of the soul through a prismatically richer imagery. No serious estimate of Baudelaire dare refuse him vision. The insight of Rimbaud–'Baudelaire est le premier voyant, roi des poètes, un *vrai Dieu'*–forbids denial. But what Rimbaud seems to have lacked was Baudelaire's persistent intuition of evil and of good. Only at the end of his brief literary life did such discernment become equally agonizing. Then he dropped poetry: *c'était mal.* Baudelaire, until he stumbled before the confessional at Namur, was a poet.

The question of his popularity, the justification of his *gloire*, is a challenge which cannot be faced in this essay. Introducing the poems in his *Situation de Baudelaire*, Valéry suggested an explanation along formal lines which a subsequent commentator, Benjamin Fondane, who died in a concentration camp before being able to revise his untidy but suggestive book, *Baudelaire et le Gouffre*, rejected as inadequate to the spiritual situation of a poet accompanied, like Pascal, with a perpetual sense of the abyss. Valéry finds the crown of Baudelaire's achievement in his having engendered some of the greatest modern French poets. One can go further and ask whether up to the time of Valéry himself any poet of distinction in France has escaped Baudelaire's influence? And Fondane caps the question with the statement that his thought is at the source of all the literary doctrines that have distracted our age.

Appreciation of a poet's work is usually on the wane when it has passed on its virtue to several generations of disciples. Yet no virtue seems to have gone out of Baudelaire. He is still in our midst, as Jacques Rivière said forty years ago. From Swinburne to Eliot, from Brunetière to Sartre, opinions clash in vehement opposition. Baudelaire remains worth discussion and, if he did not make the choice that could satisfy M Sartre, it may be because, more like Kierkegaard, his feeling of *Angst* for the human situation and his own was due to an obsession with original sin. In his fascinating *Introduction à la Poésie française*, M Thierry Maulnier has expressed reservations about including this unequal poet in the hierarchy of the purest. Like all serious French writers, and though none more than he hated obtrusive moralizing, Baudelaire is a moralist *à sa façon*, and like most serious poets he has a rhetoric of his own. His universal acceptance has rested and rests on a number of poems whose quality is as unmistakable as it is indefinable. Valéry comes as near to a hint as any admirer has yet done by insisting simply on their 'charme continu', the spell they exert: and how numerous the attractive poems are, relative to a total of less than two hundred! Nothing proves their originality more clearly than the monotonous failure of certain solemn mimicries of their effects. Even when Verlaine or Mallarmé imitated, the contrast was disturbing; when Moréas tried his ambitious hand, it was lamentable; when Rollinat devoted all his energies to the task, the result was catastrophic. An authentic cry from the vortex yields no more to pastiche than to parody and there are tones of incomparable suavity which defy cultivation.

Yet for over twenty years undercurrents of magnetism from other parts of the work have been setting in against the exclusive pull of the poems. Interest has broadened to include a keen respect for the criticism, to which art journalism in England as well as in France frequently refers for *aperçus* and support, while psychology fastens more and more firmly on the intimate writing, the diaries and letters. It is possible that the personality as expressed in the non-poetical remains now excites more curiosity and absorbs more expert attention than the poems receive. It would be excessive to say that Baudelaire survives as a 'case' rather than as a poet; but critical concentration on the accompaniments and asides of the *œuvre* has done much to sustain and deepen our interest in the poems, and is continuously correcting our evaluation of them and their author. 'The intimate notes', in the opinion of a close student of the subject, 'may appeal to us more than does the rest of the work; it is not what they say which touches us but the unconcerted simplicity with which they say it.'[1] The critic admits a danger: such fragments can be made to serve almost any thesis.

The poignant entries in the notebooks and the more abundant revelations of the correspondence have already tempted partisans and special pleaders to arrange and re-arrange their contradictory maxims, prayers, confessions, objurations, denials and maledictions according to the contention each wishes to support, forcing strange misalliances on what were detached, sporadic annotations of ambivalent moods and fluctuating impulses–the moods and impulses of one of the most acute of modern sensibilities involved in a spiritual impasse as obscure and disturbing as any which confronts psychology, and about which the poet

[1] Jean Massin: *Baudelaire: Entre Dieu et Satan*, p. 279.

himself could no more than any of his interpreters come to a right conclusion. 'Le drame de Baudelaire c'est qu'il ne peut pas conclure sainement,' says M Blin, one of the ablest of recent commentators on the poet's thought. With this bias in favour of the confessional and critical aspects, the poems are in danger of being relegated to the second shelf before the perfection of many of the less imposing of them has been widely appreciated. A florilege of surprising freshness might still be put together from the verses of Baudelaire without any of the more noxious flowers of evil figuring in the bowl. A tactful addition of one or two of the orchids or nightshades would make a ravishing bouquet. If however their charm could be analysed completely, it would almost certainly be found that the psychological element, the main objective of contemporary study, had contributed more than any other to placing the poems *hors concours*. The task is to appreciate that element, not in the mind of the man writing letters or entering notes in his diary, but as a living ingredient in his poems.

No one has yet succeeded, no one is likely to succeed, in summing up Baudelaire. He has already been many things, with conviction, to many men. One can but attempt to discover one's way of regarding him and orientate oneself as closely as possible to that. If among the hierarchy of commentators I should venture to obtrude a view of my own, it would be that the problem of Baudelaire's psychology is insoluble on the biographical plane, because there is no discernible centre of co-ordination, no unification, despite the fact that he had so definite a personality: only a carfax of conflicting and frequently self-destroying impulses, relentlessly driven to seek, and perhaps ultimately finding, the one possible resolution of their discords in the diapasons and finales of the major poems. In support of such a view the chief witness would be the poet himself, whose lucidity of conscience accompanies each step he makes along the *via dolorosa*. For nothing could be more mistaken than to think it paradoxical to insist on certain basic elements of moral intuition perceptible, not in behaviour, of which he gave no impressive example, or even in the pulse of an effective inner check, but in a revulsion of the judgment related less closely to moral codes than to spiritual sanctions which he never, though he spurned them, lost from sight. Through a life of frustrations ending in disaster, judgment and confession are sustained with a kind of heroic automatism, recurrently obstructed but resilient, issuing as from volcanic depths through stresses and tensions into a poetical and critical achievement of singular resonance and of a beauty masterfully controlled. When all reservations have been made, the impression left on most minds capable of judging the work of this bitter pessimist and profligate is one of grandeur and nobility; for all its necrological emphasis, it contributes not only an *approfondissement* but an enhancement of life.

His was indeed an ill-starred existence full of disillusions and embarrassments, early extravagances and indiscretions having involved the contraction of debts and maladies and fostered inveterate habits of procrastination. Yet the real affliction was not of course external: it lay in those warring antinomies which express themselves in the perception, dating from childhood but formulated after the manner of De Quincey, of 'l'horreur de la vie et l'extase de la vie'; or in that intimate note which Gide was fond of citing: 'Il y a dans tout homme, à toute heure, deux postulations simultanées; l'une vers Dieu, l'autre vers Satan'; or again in the practice of that dubious alchemy by which a phosphorescent poem is extracted from putrescent matter.

Corruption of the best? Personal degeneracy? 'Perversity'? Let us suspend decision until we have glanced at some of the works. This, it may be, is one of those rare poets whose *for intérieur* is the arena in which the spiritual antagonisms of their age are focussed and floodlit, and whose existence is absorbed and wrecked in a kind of atonement. Catastrophe in such a case can be a most sensitive index to the decadence of society and, when the last count is settled, the failure may be more apparent than complete: it can be transmuted into accents of baffling sublimity which suggest a conviction of irrefragable achievement and of ransom reserved:

> Je sais que vous gardez une place au Poète
> Dans les rangs bienheureux des saintes Légions
> Et que vous l'invitez à l'éternelle fête
> Des Trônes, des Vertus, des Dominations.

> Je sais que la douleur est la noblesse unique
> Où ne mordront jamais la terre et les enfers

Et qu'il faut pour tresser ma couronne mystique
Imposer tous les temps et tous les univers.[1]

*

The buffeted blossoming of Baudelaire's reputation, having survived the snubs and costs of Second Empire censorship, was, despite Saintsbury's early prediction that he was likely to appeal to the English, well nigh ruined for the Englishman's appreciation by those 'sad, bad, glad, mad' brothers of the 'Nineties, eager to flout Victorian prudery by presenting a French poet 'infinitely more perverse, morbid, exotic'[2], as if Baudelaire had come to teach depravity as a form of aestheticism or sadism as a way of life. Shipped off east for his follies he certainly had been by an angry stepfather, only to return with a more pronounced partiality for dark skins, tropical odours and tamarind trees. He was not of course the first to have had his senses sharpened by exile. And he would have been the last to feast off children's brains, as in his exquisite days he had boasted of having done at a café table to the reported perturbation of the other clients—bourgeois, no doubt, and so far from being scandalized, bored, we may be sure, by what they were meant to overhear. The fantastic over-insistence on the perversity[3] of Baudelaire became a relish for the sinfulness in which he indulged but with an abhorrence whose sincerity was hardly perceived by the generations of Swinburne and Wilde. Thus for most Englishmen Baudelaire became two contradictory things at once: the scapegoat for those who abused the arts in the name of respectability and the pure artist beyond good and evil.

But the reactions of our *fin de siècle* enthusiasts were picturesque and positive compared with the grim aloofness of the French academics. Baudelaire has had some admirable editors, expert, among other things, at extracting gems from the dust of doctoral

---

[1] English translations of the lengthier quoted passages will be found in the Appendix on page 57. For a study of this nature it has not been thought necessary to provide translations of all the shorter quotations.   [2] Arthur Symons, quoted by Mr T. S. Eliot in his essay on Baudelaire in *Selected Essays*.   [3] Note the frequency with which such terms of abuse were used in nineteenth-century criticism: 'The truth is that Mr Wordsworth with all his perversities is a person of great powers . . . There are scattered up and down the book, and in the midst of the most repulsive portions (*sic*), a very great number of lines and images that sparkle like gems in the dust.' (Jeffrey).

theses, many of them lying like withered wreaths on the head of the poet's grave. Light on such cases of psychological and artistic subtlety as this has come slowly enough under the régime of insensitiveness characteristic of the official study of French literature for a good half-century. In 1892 Brunetière denounced the project to raise a statue to Baudelaire as 'ériger en exemple la débauche et l'immoralité.' The fulminating moralist was still at that stage in the estimate of *Les Fleurs du Mal* which could condemn separate poems detached from their context as the character of Iago might be condemned if isolated from the play. And though the critic's disapproval of this 'Belzébuth de table d'hôte' became less certain of itself as the unheeding public of taste continued to read the poems, his appreciation advanced no further than the historian's view that the *point de départ* for the Symbolist movement was to be sought in one of Baudelaire's sonnets. As for Lanson, the division of labour which has tended to separate methodical scholarship from literary discernment has gone far to destroy its object when so eminent a historian of literature could write, 'La sensibilité est nulle chez Baudelaire: sauf une exception.'[1] The *Tableaux Parisiens*, in which, to apply Mr Eliot's words, imagery of the sordid life of a great metropolis is elevated to the *first intensity*, were for Lanson 'de la peinture inutile', 'painting to no purpose'. His verdict on the poet ends with this remark: 'Par sa bizarrerie voulue et puissante, mais aussi par sa facture magistrale Baudelaire a exercé une influence considérable.' Contemporary masters of the bizarre do not seem to find much room for Baudelaire in their tradition. What modern poetry owes to him most is the extended sense and use of analogy.[2]

Writing to his junior early in 1862 Alfred de Vigny insisted that for him many of the *Fleurs du Mal* were 'Fleurs du bien'; he regretted the 'unworthy title' and reproached the author for having poisoned the book with vague emanations from the cemetery of Hamlet. A rank odour of sensationalism transmitted through the turgid tradition of melodrama and the *roman noir*, if not from the crypts of Elsinore at least from the dungeons of Otranto, mars some of Baudelaire's strongest poems. To accept the title (hastily substituted for *Les Limbes*) as an indication of

---

[1] This curious phrase comes from the *Histoire de la Littérature française*. The exception appears to be death. [2] Even Faguet fell short. See Gide's stinging retort: 'Baudelaire et M Faguet' (*Morceaux Choisis*).

the nature and spirit of every piece in the collection, or even of most, would be an initial mistake–'ce titre ridicule', as M Thierry Maulnier complains with a gesture of impatience at the 'satanisme à bon marché' it suggests.

Part of Baudelaire's originality lies in his intimate variety, the range of which can remain unrecognized even by those who are familiar with his poems. For the notion, propagated by the poet himself, of the *mauvais moine*, the procrastinator of genius, fluctuating between the limbos of horror and ecstasy and spasmodically precipitating an occasional poem of strange power and unaccountable finish, is as inadequate applied to the man as it appears when confronted by the series of his collected works in a contemporary edition. The prose is so far free from taint that one can insist on the very different tone of the extra-poetical writings. The poet and the diarist concentrate on an intimate problem; the critic displays a comparatively serene objectivity. And what nineteenth-century critic has written with an equal degree of brilliant distinction and care? Pater's distinction has not the ease of Baudelaire's, whose prose in its controlled vigour and effortless balance reminds one at times of Newman's. Not imposing in quantity though by no means sparse, Baudelaire's criticism has the novelty of being expert in two arts, literature and painting, and original in combining attention to them with fruitful reactions to music. In the three genres, though often preoccupied with minor figures, he excels in the application of creative intuition to characteristic specimens and effective theorizing. The piece on Victor Hugo in the *Réflexions sur quelques-uns de mes Contemporains* is the richest and most sustained of all his literary studies. Good, but in a different vein, is the short treatment of *Madame Bovary*, with which Flaubert was delighted. Yet the masterpiece is surely *Le Peintre de la Vie moderne*, the sequence that centres in the work of Constantin Guys.

To characterize precisely the technique of these studies would not be easy. To read them is to recover a sense of the lost art of good writing, set off with some of the virtues of French style: discrimination, lightness with gravity, elegance, a touch of rhetoric, something of that indefinable spell, considered by Valéry as the differentia of the poetry; and for all their subtleties and digressions, how readable, how intelligible they are! Baudelaire's aesthetic thinking is of an intuitive, not the philosophical, kind,

14

yet often theoretical; a species of generalization starting from an interview, a masterpiece, an *œuvre*, and developing into an interpretation full of acute characterizations or profound formulas, exceeding the example in scope and significance; not practical criticism in the contemporary sense (some of Baudelaire's approbations would not be accredited today), but predominantly positive, the expression of 'admiration' with 'reasons' adduced in support. Baudelaire was capable of fervour.

It has been suggested that the criticism represents a desperately successful effort to compensate for the personal tragedy revealed in the poems. But fine work cannot be produced by a subterfuge. The querulous moralist might object that *Les Paradis Artificiels* are in prose. But are these more obnoxious than the confessions of that other Opium Eater, on which they were modelled? Both works prompt speculations that transcend intoxicants; and the responsive reader may be relied on to confirm the harmlessness, if not the innocence, of the *Poème du Haschisch*.

Baudelaire did not murder or steal as Villon is accused of having done. He failed to keep pace with his debts, and this was a major anxiety, though he died with some of his inheritance withheld safe in the hands of the family solicitor, so safe in fact that the solicitor's descendants are reported to have found insuperable difficulties in parting with the residue. As for his vices, those on record are scarcely unusual according to the standards of our time. He had a mistress who was a mulatto and a low comedienne; she was rather stupid and in no sense temperate. It is rumoured that on one occasion at least he pommelled the floor of her flat with her head. But her hair was luxuriant and odorous: it inspired one of his most nostalgic poems. He railed rather peevishly against her in one of his letters to his mother, as 'a creature *who doesn't admire me,* and who has no interest even in my studies, who would throw my manuscripts on the fire, if that could bring her in more money than by allowing them to be published.' In another letter he reproached himself grievously with having ruined her twice in his own interest while she suffered in silence. He strove to make amends and to succour her even in his final affliction. His friends thought she lacked beauty and scoffed at his fidelity. But when they spoke ill of her his genius rebounded and avenged her in this magnificent and ambiguous sonnet:

15

Je te donne ces vers afin que si mon nom
Aborde heureusement aux époques lointaines,
Et fait rêver un soir les cervelles humaines,
Vaisseau favorisé par un grand aquilon,

Ta mémoire, pareille aux fables incertaines,
Fatigue le lecteur ainsi qu'un tympanon,
Et par un fraternel et mystique chaînon
Reste comme pendu à mes rimes hautaines;

Être maudit à qui, de l'abîme profond
Jusqu'au plus haut du ciel, rien, hors moi ne répond!
— O toi qui, comme une ombre à la trace éphémère,

Foules d'un pied léger et d'un regard serein
Les stupides mortels qui t'ont jugée amère,
Statue aux yeux de jais, grand ange au front d'airain!

That was the Black Venus; there was a white one. Mme Sabatier was described by Gautier as a woman of rare and splendid beauty. To her salon of admirers she was 'La Présidente'. Wits took fire at her glance. Clésinger struck marble into the curves of her nudity and made a sensation with 'La Femme au Serpent'. She sat for many portraits. The equivocal but not unhappy passion she inspired in the poet has been called 'platonic', though platonism was not her forte. It is known she possessed a little pencil drawing of her abominated rival, which he must have given her. On it she had scribbled: 'Son idéal!' Then there was 'La Belle aux Cheveux d'Or.' Marie Daubrun was a pretty actress with a genuine talent. A charming account has been written of her relationship with the poet[1]; the purest lyrical notes awakened at her touch. There was also Berthe, Agathe, and that 'modiste érudite et dévote' for whom he wrote *Franciscae Meae Laudes*. And was there a separate identity behind the initials 'J.F.G.'? Jeanne Duval remained the loadstone. In cadaveresque embrace against 'l'affreuse Juive' he longs for the noble physique and cold eyes of his mistress. The circle of his bondage is soon closed. Baudelaire was hardly a Casanova for promiscuity.

[1] Albert Feuillerat: *Baudelaire et la Belle aux Cheveux d'Or.*

Yet Fondane is right; he was a brutal sensualist. Eroticism was the confessed symbol of his guilt: the motif of corrupt carnality recurs repulsively through his life, thought and work. What surprises one is how much of his work and thought, if not of his life, escaped its thrall. I had forgotten that, having attempted suicide, he wrote up an ironic account of the event which sounds more sincere than the references to it in one of his letters: 'I am killing myself because I am useless to others and dangerous to myself . . . because I am immortal and because I HOPE . . . Point out to her (to Jeanne) my dreadful example and how disorder of mind and life leads to sombre despair and complete annihilation.' He struck himself with a knife and woke up at the *commissariat de police* whence, after receiving a scolding, he was carried home. His mother was gracious and copied out his verses; but she drank bordeaux whereas he liked burgundy. It has been suggested that the scene was arranged to persuade General Aupick to pay off his stepson's notorious debts.

All this is neither edifying nor exceptional. Such predicaments and depravities are common in 'Bohemia', a term that was coming into vogue in Baudelaire's youth to characterize the post-patronage community of poets and artists. His personal luck is persistently bad, which means that if it takes a turn for the better he misses the turn; he is, as Mr Eliot has said, a bungler. What is exceptional in Baudelaire, apart from the fact that he is a poet, is his extraordinary sense of guilt. In adding profundity to his vision, it communicates an incomparable tremor to his verse. His poems reflect in their depths not a mere 'frisson macabre' but a 'tempête sous un crâne.'

To an age of psychoanalysis a sense of guilt is also something of a commonplace. There seems no good reason for rejecting the help offered by the theory of the Œdipus Complex, provided we recognize the limits of its application. Analysis produces a useful formulation of certain aspects of Baudelaire's inner conflict, which it assimilates to a well identified neurotic pattern. This, according to our tastes, we may accept or reject in favour of the opposition theory of M Sartre. Baudelaire's father, an attractive man of some artistic attainment, had married at sixty and had died when his child was six. The boy's passion for his mother, later referred to in the most explicit terms, was thwarted and envenomed by her marriage to an officer who was promoted to

17

a high rank and became French ambassador at Constantinople. The antipathy Charles felt for his stepfather was so marked that during the political excitement of '48, the poet rushed about the barricades flourishing a rifle and crying: 'Il faut fusiller le général Aupick!' Such facts speak nowadays for more than themselves. Science assimilates to type. But the images of a poet are unpredictable and differentiate a special sensibility. The singularity of this case cannot be fully explained—can it even be isolated?—without intelligent reference to the major function, to the poems of a mind conditioned as much by the religious orientations as by the personal *rapports* of his childhood.

It becomes clear that Baudelaire's deeper *états d'âme* are rooted, not in Catholic aestheticism—although he makes much use of ritualistic imagery—but in dogma; at least in some of the explicit fundamentals of the Catholic faith. How to define his religious attitude is a question of endless discussion. The Belgian poet, Georges Rodenbach, claimed with ingenuous confidence that he was a Catholic poet. The Catholic critic, Brunetière, denounced him as a 'Satan d'hôtel garni'. Léon Cladel, who called Baudelaire his master, considered his claim to be ultramontane as 'pur Dandysme'. In the most serious study of the poet's religion that has appeared, *Baudelaire: Entre Dieu et Satan*, M Jean Massin speaks of his 'drôle de Christianisme' as 'that of a sinner who knows himself to be a sinner.' (Not a bad qualification for Christian candidature, one would suppose.) Himself a Catholic whose sympathy for the poems is genuine, M Massin refuses to confirm the canonization of 'Saint Charles Baudelaire,' and is content to believe that the poet was at all times 'impregnated with Christianity,' striving to become a more virtuous, if not a more orthodox, Christian. 'To make Baudelaire a perfect catholic,' he adds, 'is not only to betray him but to betray catholicism.' Yet the poet often referred to himself as a catholic—once, for instance, in protest, on hearing from his mother that, when she had passed a copy of *Les Fleurs du Mal* to the *curé* of Honfleur, that sensitive cleric had pitched it on the fire. On another occasion he complained to a fellow poet that Chenavard had 'never scented the catholic beneath the *Fleurs du Mal*, in which he was certainly wrong, for does anyone exist more catholic than the devil?' And to speak of Baudelaire's contemporaries, it is when we compare his attitude with the aggressively anti-catholic

18

and anti-christian attitude of Leconte de Lisle or with the pan-
theistic Manicheism of Hugo, that it is seen to differ *toto cœlo*
from theirs.

Confronted by this impenetralia of theological subtleties and
refinements, the lay critic might be content to conclude that
Baudelaire was a man fascinated by mystical perspectives at
which he gazed through Roman lenses, without being able to
find his feet in orthodoxy. Even his most sympathetic admirers
seem to have had doubts. Warmhearted Barbey d'Aurevilly,
self-appointed Connétable des Lettres and flamboyant defender
of the Faith, concluded a famous review with the remark: 'Only
two decisions are open to the poet who wrote *Les Fleurs du Mal:*
to become a Christian or to blow out his brains.' And Paul
Bourget, who recovered at a late hour from the analysis of liber-
tinage in the novel to end his days in the odour of sanctity, could
speak of Baudelaire as a 'catholique désabusé devenu un libertin
analysateur.'

There seems no reason to doubt that, from infancy, Baudelaire
had acquired a religious conception of life and the universe which
remained, unaffected by his backslidings and blasphemies, the
mainspring of his spiritual aspirations. To say he could not shake
himself free from certain dogmas would understate the case: for
him they were axiomatic, shaped out of the logic of existence.
Feeling, imagination, and intermittently but profoundly thought
itself were in his case conditioned by, 'impregnated with', the
Catholic conception of God, the Devil, angels, hell, purgatory,
heaven. In moments of blasphemy any of these might be denied
except the Devil, in whose person and presence he seems to have
believed with a conviction compared with which Gide's was
that of a recent convert. His notions of original and actual sin
are, says M Massin, Christian, but his conception of redemption
is much less clear; his knowledge of Christ is inadequate: 'tra-
gique ignorance du Sauveur.' Massin finds Baudelaire devoted
to a salvation of self-help: 'his mind avows itself incapable of
communion, imprisoned in the desire for personal realization.'
But there is not apparently a passage in his works which denies
a single dogma of the Church explicitly. In any interpretation of
society and the universe which is not related to Catholic assump-
tions he shows no kind of interest, none in science or progress or
democracy.

Emile Verhaeren, one of his numerous progeny who was capti-
vated by these things, used to complain that he could not shake
off 'ce vieux fonds de catholicisme.' That would be true of
Baudelaire without the complaint. Yet what he cannot or will
not do is to conform to its injunctions. At times he seems to
profess a dismal kind of delight in this disability and his self-
indulgence becomes deliberate. Here is his perversity and he
knows it not as a literary affectation, but as *sin*, an attitude of the
soul. His plight is abject and not without complicity, but there
is no shade of falsehood in his clairvoyance. Of some of his
poems Fondane says, 'Vice, that double fault against morals and
taste, displays itself in them and ambitiously claims spiritual
primacy; and what is worse, with a kind of conviction.' Remorse
ensues, not repentance, remorse for procrastination. The cry,
too late! the realization of the irremediable, strikes harrowing
tones of melodious anguish out of his instrument, such as had not
been heard in French poetry since Racine. Ennui, the accom-
plice of despair, supervenes; and yielding to that travesty of
mysticism to which certain temperaments are prone, his religious impulses are diverted into 'erotology', to be in turn thwarted
by his lucidity, his logical sense of degradation, and finally
precipitated, analysed and fixed, in a little marvel of subtle form,
one of those 'poèmes noirs et splendides qui comptent', as
Thierry Maulnier says, 'parmi les plus beaux de nos lettres':

> Tête-à-tête sombre et limpide
> Qu'un cœur devenu son miroir!
> Puits de Vérité, clair et noir,
> Où tremble une étoile livide,
>
> Un phare ironique, infernal,
> Flambeau des grâces sataniques,
> Soulagement et gloire uniques,
> – La conscience dans le Mal!

La conscience dans le Mal: is his special awareness of evil the secret
of Baudelaire? If so perhaps the difference between him and ourselves, *hypocrite lecteur*, is that he faced his Judgment before the
time. On the state of mind revealed here it would be better not
to comment since one spiritual expert has left it to Divine Mercy

to assess. Let us take our last word from the poet himself: 'il était impossible de faire autrement *l'agitation de l'esprit dans le mal.*' This he conceives as his appointed task. Its execution involves the experience of great suffering, and the analysis of suffering in himself and in others is the saving theme of the deeper poems. Sainte-Beuve, whose attitude was sympathetic to the person of the poet, whereas what the poet needed and begged for was a public expression of interest in his work, put his finger on the problem in a letter written after receiving a copy of *Les Fleurs du Mal:* 'Et vous avez pris l'Enfer, vous vous êtes fait Diable . . . en pétrarquisant sur l'horrible, vous avez l'air de vous être joué, vous avez pourtant souffert, – *vous avez dû beaucoup souffrir,* mon pauvre enfant!' L'Oncle Beuve knew something about it. Had he not withdrawn his toes from the same sulphurous sea? His young *protégé* had unwisely plunged in and was caught struggling in the eddies without help. Yet it is at this vortex-depth of torment that Baudelaire's larger hope begins to operate through the conviction that suffering is the poet's ransom, reinstates the vision of the Celestial Hierarchy and 'prepares a place':

Je sais que vous gardez une place au Poète . . .

That the whole argumentation has been pronounced unorthodox may be a serious theological charge. But most readers would agree that the theme of suffering to which Baudelaire so often returned has produced stanzas of such compassionate beauty and power that few in modern poetry can be compared with them in breadth and poignancy of sympathy:

C'est un cri répété par mille sentinelles,
Un ordre renvoyé par mille porte-voix;
C'est un phare allumé sur mille citadelles,
Un appel de chasseurs perdus dans les grands bois!

Car c'est vraiment, Seigneur, le meilleur témoignage
Que nous puissions donner de notre dignité
Que cet ardent sanglot qui roule d'âge en âge
Et vient mourir au bord de votre éternité!

And for those to whom these tragic sublimities have become

familiar, there is the prodigious conclusion of the poet's meditation on the fate of 'Les Petites Vieilles':

> Ruines! ma famille! ô cerveaux congénères!
> Je vous fais chaque soir un solennel adieu!
> Où serez-vous demain, Èves octogénaires,
> Sur qui pèse la griffe effroyable de Dieu?

*

In one of his essays on the poet Mr Eliot suggests that 'the opinion that Baudelaire was an artist exclusively for art's sake' had obstructed a proper judgment. The poet, he says, 'came into vogue at a time when "Art for Art's sake" was a dogma'. The authority of Gautier could be cited in support of this view: 'Baudelaire was for the absolute autonomy of art and could not admit that the poem had any other end but itself or any other mission but to excite in the reader the sensation of the beautiful in the absolute sense of the term'. But the error is not merely referable to the time in which these poets lived. Baudelaire, the aesthetician, must bear some degree of direct responsibility for a confusion of issues and terms which cannot be straightened out here, though the nature of the misconception may briefly be indicated.

Although his allegiance blew hot and cold, it is doubtful whether at any time Baudelaire subscribed to the doctrine as expounded by Gautier, except to acquiesce on the negative side in an amoral attitude adopted in defence of art against didacticism. The origins of Art for Art's sake lie in the artist's active experience, and the notion recurs perennially, fusing the practice of good craftsmanship with the perception of the 'Vie des Formes' and the finer aspects of taste. Its formulation in the second quarter of the nineteenth century marks a reaction from romantic Messianism, on the one hand, and on the other, from the prohibitions of bourgeois philistinism: poetry is design, the lyric is a verbal cameo or enamel. This emphasis was fundamental to the Parnassian idea of the 'plastic', against which Baudelaire himself protested in a vehement article, putting the case for humane literature against the excessive devotion of his contemporaries to paganism in stone. Elsewhere however he confessed that he had be'en attracted to 'the plastic' from infancy, and he resorts to the word whenever he needs it. Much of his imagery conforms to the type.

His insistence on the autonomy of poetry was derived in the form in which he expressed it, not from Théophile Gautier, but from Edgar Allan Poe's essay on the *Poetic Principle* which, surprising as it might seem, has had a fortune in France that makes one think at times of the role of Coleridge's *Biographia Literaria* in English romanticism or even of the *Symposium* in the Renaissance. A phrase like 'La poésie, pour peu qu'on veuille descendre en soi-même, interroger son âme, rappeler ses souvenirs d'enthousiasme, n'a pas d'autre but qu'elle-même; elle ne peut pas en avoir d'autre, et aucun poëme ne sera si grand, si noble, si véritablement digne du nom de poëme, que celui qui aura été écrit uniquement pour le plaisir d'écrire un poëme' is an embellished adaptation, along with much else in his articles on the American, which has been accepted as part of the French poet's aesthetic creed. Actually what Baudelaire appropriated from Poe was assimilated with all the more ease since his own conception of poetry was equally idealistic. Both poets are with Gautier in agreement over anti-didacticism and anti-philistinism, but with this difference. Poe and Baudelaire tend towards a *mysticisme d'art* related to a supernatural conception of Beauty. For *le bon Théo* the external world exists and the artist's job is not to interpret it mystically but, as Mallarmé implied in his *Toast Funèbre*, to give it the one form of permanence which is real: the precarious eternity of art. Whereas for Poe, poetry needs no justification; it exists in its own right as a reflection of ultimate Beauty. In his discussion of the Poetic Principle Poe had said, 'while this Principle itself is, strictly and simply, the Human Aspiration for Supernal Beauty, the manifestation of the Principle is always found in *an elevating excitement of the Soul*–quite independent of that passion which is the intoxication of the Heart–or of that Truth which is the satisfaction of the Reason'.

Obviously Poe's conception soars above moralistic justification as smoothly as Gautier's evades it. But, and this requires emphasis, the *impartial* force of both lines of argument is lost if they are used as excuses for immorality in art. Such a notion could never have occurred to the great three. Art for the sake of licence was a fiction of the smaller fry of censors and imitators who snapped

23

and chattered at their heels. And in England Swinburne and Wilde did more to queer than to clear the pitch.

Mr Eliot is none the less right to ignore Baudelaire's contention that when he wrote a poem it was with the sole object of writing a poem. The impulse to create a beautiful pattern of irresponsible words seized him frequently, no doubt, with results to be appraised later in this essay. But such an objective could not possibly account for a collection as various in type and so rich in significance as *Les Fleurs du Mal*. 'Who', asks M Massin, 'could be persuaded to believe that the finest, the saddest and the most human poems of the collection owe their existence to preoccupations of a strictly aesthetic order?' At times Baudelaire declared the intention of the work to be purely aesthetic; at times he foreswore himself vigorously. The whole truth seems to have emerged in a burst of self-justification addressed to Ancelle, the family solicitor: 'Faut-il vous dire que dans ce livre *atroce* j'ai mis tout *mon cœur*, toute *ma tendresse*, toute *ma religion* (travestie), toute *ma haine*? Il est vrai que j'écrirai le contraire; que je jurerai mes grands dieux que c'est un livre *d'art pur*, de *singerie*, de *jonglerie;* et je mentirai comme un arracheur de dents'.

Despite his support of the claims of pure poetry, Baudelaire is a *poète engagé*. But let us not flatter ourselves that the apparent contradictions in his mind can be smoothed out with a phrase. We must glance at another aspect of the conflict. Baudelaire is in conscious revolt against much in the practice of his predecessors. Not against Romanticism. How could he have been in complete revolt against the literary Zeitgeist, of which he left one of the best definitions?–'Qui dit romantisme dit art moderne, c'est-à-dire intimité, spiritualité, couleur, aspiration vers l'infini, exprimées par tous les moyens que contiennent les arts'. Actually he had outdistanced his contemporaries, by having, as Sainte-Beuve said, gone off in a wherry to Kamchatka. What he strongly disapproved of was the reliance his predecessors had placed on 'orgiastic' inspiration and their indifference to control of the means of art. 'L'orgie n'est pas la sœur de l'inspiration; nous avons cessé cette parenté adultère . . .' A more subtle distinction is drawn in one of the sketches for a preface to the poems: 'Des poètes illustres s'étaient partagé depuis longtemps les provinces les plus fleuries du domaine poëtique. Il m'a paru plaisant et d'autant plus agréable que la tâche était plus difficile, d'extraire

24

la *beauté du Mal*. Ce livre, essentiellement inutile et absolument innocent, n'a pas été fait dans un autre but que de me divertir et d'exercer mon goût prononcé pour l'obstacle'. Here the extraction of beauty from evil is regarded in terms of the aesthetic pleasure derived from *la difficulté vaincue*, under the aegis of Gautier's famous 'inutile'. But there is more in it than that. Mr Eliot spoke of the care Baudelaire took with his poems. Such scrupulousness was part of the genuine reaction of poets of his time from those who had thought it enough to look into their hearts to write. Baudelaire's concern went beyond this. As Rimbaud was to perceive, he was creating a new visionary art. Allowances must be made for his fluctuations between the formal and the speculative purposiveness.

We must also allow for the fluctuations of his critics. Sainte-Beuve, in the passage already quoted, saw from the first the novel and perilous ambition of the work: 'Et vous avez pris l'Enfer . . .' Valéry ignores the *dessous*, when he describes the dominant impulse as 'le désir, en un mot, d'une substance plus solide et d'une forme plus savante et plus pure'. Benjamin Fondane settled the matter as justly as it is capable of being settled and placed the argument in the right perspective. Referring to the poems, 'Leur *pourquoi*', he said, 'nous révèlera encore une fois, s'il en était besoin, que ce n'est pas d'une méditation sur le fait littéraire qu'elles sont issues, mais d'une expérience intense, métaphysique, religieuse dont le fait littéraire n'est que l'ultime et intelligente expression, déguisée.'

Baudelaire believed in justification by the arts. To refuse this form of good works was for the artist the unforgivable sin: '. . . et qui ont refusé la Rédemption par le travail'. M Jean Massin makes a grave comment on this attitude: 'The admirable honesty with which Baudelaire devotes himself to his task and duty as poet induces him to consider poetry as a second way to redemption alongside the primary. It is not possible to follow him in this direction'. All this serious critic finds to condone is the fact that Baudelaire made no attempt to gain redemption by using his art for such 'missions' as those the Romanticists undertook: to play the Magus or moral guide of mankind or the reformer of society like Hugo or Vigny's Chatterton. A layman intruding in these matters risks sophistry, perhaps even damnation. But he may not feel sure that the poet's case has been fully stated. Let us approach the problem of justification from a different angle by asking what are the sins which Baudelaire appears to dread most? In *his* order of gravity they are profligacy, procrastination and ennui, his personal form of 'l'acedia, maladie des moines', that connivance in despair which saps resistance and frustrates energy. But profligacy, procrastination and frustration in relation to what? His appointed task as a poet can be the only valid answer. And what were the dimensions of the task? Was the critic who accused Victor Hugo of being 'un grand poëte scriptural qui a l'œil fermé à la spiritualité'–a poet 'in whom God in a mood of inscrutable mystification had fused stupidity with genius'–was Baudelaire himself endowed with such potentialities as could have made him the great modern French poet Hugo was not? If his evasions and indulgences obstruct the development of his art, is it unnatural of him to express, not fear of losing his soul (which he never expressed) but anxiety about impairing his talents and missing redemption through failing to complete his task? The problem can be given a more realistic turn if we ask simply what Baudelaire could have done, *had he had more time*, that is had he not hastened his own end? M Massin raises this question. But the implication of his treatment seems to be that the poet attempted to *compensate* through his art for the failure of his life. Whereas for Baudelaire such a 'distinction' could only have been confusing; the value of life and the value of art were *for him* one; his failure in each is one and the same failure. But the fragments of poetic achievement salvaged from the ruins amount none the less to a spiritual achievement:

. . . j'ai fait mon devoir
Comme un parfait chimiste et comme une âme sainte.

Whatever we make of Baudelaire, it seems impossible to explain any of his views without admitting that the most important of them assume spiritual values. We cannot hope to understand his view of poetry in particular, if we fail to perceive that he regarded it as a supernatural gift. Such conviction he expressed repeatedly: 'La Poésie est ce qu'il y a de plus réel, c'est ce qui n'est complètement vrai que dans *un autre monde*. Ce monde-ci, dictionnaire hiéroglyphique'. The latter phrase he took from the lips of his ideal painter, Eugène Delacroix. But he adapted it to a system of quasi-mystical thought which for several generations had been exerting an influence on the imagination of Western Europe, the extent of which is not even now fully appreciated.[1]

The eccentricities of Baudelaire's catholicism have more than once been related to the tradition of *literary* catholicism which passes through Chateaubriand and Joseph de Maistre down to the Amaury of Sainte-Beuve's *Volupté*. In his fragmentary journal, *Mon Cœur mis à nu*, Baudelaire confessed that de Maistre and Edgar Allan Poe had taught him to think. De Maistre was that anti-revolutionary autocrat whom the King of Sardinia appointed envoy extraordinary to the court of Saint Petersburg, a champion of the Catholic hierarchy, whose catholicism was not free from a taint of Illuminism contracted through an interest in freemasonry. For Baudelaire Joseph de Maistre was a 'grand esprit'. Traces of his thought are found in several of the poems. His writings were however only one of the channels through which the poet imbibed his share of those circumambient forms of supernatural speculation, bequeathed by the revolutionary period, which sooner or later led him back to Emanuel Swedenborg. It is probable that some of Balzac's novels, almost certainly *Séraphîta*, may have directed the poet's attention in the first instance to the elaborate system of the Swedish visionary, with whose dogmatic epitome, *Heaven and Hell*, he seems to have been directly acquainted. That a doctrine expressed with so much 'matter-of-factness' could have influenced several generations of poets and artists may seem as odd to us as it did to De Quincey. But it has long been apparent that modern poetry and the other arts have absorbed much imagery of an occult or mystical cast from sources outside the classical and biblical traditions. 'We have come to give you metaphors for your poetry', declared the unknown instructors to W. B. Yeats, as he tells us in *A Vision*. Images of this provenance were adopted by Baudelaire usually from the manipulative hands of Balzac, Gérard de Nerval or Joseph de Maistre. But more firmly than any of them he accepted the doctrine of Correspondence, which relates the things of time and sense with absolute rigour to their counterparts on one plane or another of the spirit-world with which Swedenborg professed to be familiar. The real attraction of the doctrine is that it offers

[1] A fuller treatment of this subject will be found in some studies of *The Background of Modern French Poetry* to appear shortly from the Cambridge University Press.

with complete assurance and elaborate 'proof' a system of universal analogy.

With his genius for turning the thought and example of other men into something effective of his own, Baudelaire assimilates Swedenborg's notion of Correspondence to the experience of poetry and the arts. The 'celebrated' sonnet, *Correspondances*, has been called an 'aesthetic catechism'. Swedenborg was no aesthetician, but some of his ideas fit as readily as Poe's into an idealistic conception of the arts. In the following passage from his third essay on the American Baudelaire blends both sources: 'C'est cet admirable, cet immortel instinct du Beau qui nous fait considérer la terre et ses spectacles comme un aperçu, comme une correspondance du Ciel'.

In several other passages of his criticism Baudelaire involves Swedenborg's explicit authority at important junctures in the exposition of his own aesthetic. His application of the doctrine he explains most clearly of all in one of his two essays on Victor Hugo. The images of a great poet (and he applies the conception elsewhere to Gautier and to Wagner) attract and convince because they are spiritually true: such images are perceptions of universal analogies; they are 'mathematically' exact: 'Chez les excellents poètes, il n'y a pas de métaphore, de comparaison ou d'épithète qui ne soit d'une adaptation mathématiquement exacte dans la circonstance actuelle, parce que ces comparaisons, ces métaphores et ces épithètes sont puisées dans l'inépuisable fonds de l'*universelle analogie*, et qu'elles ne peuvent être puisées ailleurs.'

In this conception of the poet's function, not as prophet of a new dispensation but as 'decipherer' of the divine hieroglyphics, Baudelaire finds at once the true vocation of the poet and the differentia of his genius. Is it therefore illogical of him to see in the poetic function, not only a divine gift, but a means of justification?–

> Anges revêtus d'or, de pourpre et d'hyacinthe,
> O vous, soyez témoins que j'ai fait mon devoir
> Comme un parfait chimiste et comme une âme sainte.

The acute sense of spiritual obligation is rarely accompanied in Baudelaire's mind by a sense of duty fulfilled, and there is probably more supplication than assurance in this appeal. It is in the frustration he felt in his highest function that we find the

brunt of his tragedy. Into the origins of his psychological predicament we make no pretence to see beyond a chaos of impulses.
Montaigne was inspired to begin writing his Essays by the
'chimeras' he found 'playing the runaway horse' in the disorder
of his mind. A close comparison with Baudelaire is not suggested.
But we may now turn to observe how, having by 1857 written
most of his best poems, he attempted to present them in a
significant sequence. Opinions differ as to how far *Les Fleurs du
Mal* were planned in consecutive detail. Gustave Kahn rejected
the view. M Albert Feuillerat, to whom we are indebted for his
revelations of how Marcel Proust composed his novel, believes
that Baudelaire arranged his poems according to preoccupations
of the nicest precision. Here we shall be content to indicate
something of the significance of the main subdivisions with the
help of reference to characteristic poems. Ultimately the test of
every poet lies not in the manner of his life or in the nature of his
thought, but in what he writes down. As with many modern
poets Baudelaire's reputation has suffered from too much biographical detection. One mystery remains intact: how such a
man could rise into the heaven of art effortlessly, as if on arch-
angelic wings, yet casting a shadow.

II

THE ARCHITECTURE OF 'LES FLEURS DU MAL'

The first edition of *Les Fleurs du Mal* was a collection showing
a different arrangement and balance from the disposition of
subsequent issues. The important section called *Tableaux Parisiens*
did not exist: most of its best poems were awaiting the stimulus
of the condemnation to be written. The law can find itself in an
awkward position when confronted by an original work of art or
literature. It has usually to judge the effect as good or bad in
relation to contemporary moral standards. The incidence of
such a judgment must fall on the content narrowly conceived,
regarded in fact as an indifferent public sees it and not for what
it is worth in the context of the work. The composition is not
accepted as an ensemble, a synthesis, but is interrogated and may
be condemned on a paraphrase, an abstraction from the whole.

29

There is a touch of acute pathos in the anxiety Baudelaire showed when he appealed to that other intensely serious poet, Alfred de Vigny, on sending him the volume, to recognize that it was not a mere album and that it had a beginning and an end. Let us try to obey this injunction or at least to emulate the attitude of unbiased intelligence, which was the response made by the most distinguished judge the younger poet could have found among his elders. First, however, let us remind ourselves of the complexities of the work before us–not only the complexity of the author's mind, but the variety of interests reflected and condensed within a range of less than two hundred of his poems.[1] The tensions and attractions in conflict under the surface of this series of controlled stanza- and sonnet-forms have already inspired volumes of exegesis. Here we shall have time only to comment on the major aspects of the composition. Of these the first corresponds to the largest subdivision, *Spleen et Idéal* which, with the second, *Tableaux Parisiens*, dominates all subsequent arrangements. They are by far the most inclusive and characteristic sections, though a few poems as important as any occur in the subdivisions that follow.

The volume is dedicated to Théophile Gautier in a phrase whose grandiloquence has puzzled many of Baudelaire's admirers. Contemporary estimates of the poetry of Gautier make the tribute seem excessive, yet there are reasons for not regarding it as insincere. Gautier was a master-technician. Mr Eliot's respect for Mr Pound may throw some light on the relationship. But Baudelaire's admiration was not confined to that amazing intuition into all the arts of luxury which he found transposed in the audacious hedonism of *Mademoiselle de Maupin* or realized in the mature miniature-work of *Emaux et Camées*. Gautier was, to use a word concocted in this century, the 'imagist' *par excellence*, that is, for Baudelaire, one of the decipherers of the divine hieroglyphics and therefore a great poet; nor was Gautier himself as much averse as might appear to mystical conceptions of the poet's function.[2] Robust and genial, wearing his panoply of talents with a nonchalance free from conscious vanity, the author

[1] Cognisance should be taken of the *Petits Poèmes en Prose* collected posthumously in 1869; but space will not allow of a separate treatment of these which extend the range of the poems in verse. [2] See the chapter on Gautier in Georges Poulet: *Etudes sur le Temps humain*.

of *Emaux et Camées*, while he in turn regarded Baudelaire with conspicuous sympathy and penetration, does not seem to have perceived the superiority of *Les Fleurs du Mal*, and could scarcely have thought the dedication an exaggerated compliment.

The flattering mood ends abruptly. Nothing could more forcibly illustrate the bi-polarity of Baudelaire's mental processes than to find that he has turned from obeisance to his 'très-cher et très-vénéré maître et ami' to address the 'hypocritical reader', you and me, in what must be the most uningratiating apostrophe ever prefixed to a notable volume of verse. The curious spiritual moralist who is one of the author's *personae* accuses us of some of the worst sins humanity can commit. Our crimes and vices may be social but the judgment is of the heart of man, desperately wicked. The tone, however, is ironical, cynical, Faustian, not biblical. Each quatrain closes with a clinch of accusation, truculent in its realism or insinuating in its bitter satire. The deadliest of sins is none of the orthodox seven. It is ennui, the sin of acquiescence in spiritual defeatism, and most serious of all, the defeatism of the artist. For need it be said, the incidence of the judgment is in the last resort subjective: the censure is a *mea culpa*.

As we pass from *Au Lecteur* to *Bénédiction* we perceive the antithesis from which the tragic interest of the entire series draws its strongest effects–the judgment of man in error under the curse: the magnification of art as a supernatural and vicarious grace. That the artist has a chance of redemption through pleading the cause of mankind in the anguish of its predicament is the positive implication of his task. And this faith is the intermittent rainbow against that 'thick shadow of cloud and fire of molten light' in which Swinburne found the poems to be steeped.

Spleen et Idéal elaborates and diversifies this fundamental contrast to the extent of two-thirds of the whole collection. In *Bénédiction* the position of the poet in society is contrasted with his divine function. The poet belongs to the spiritual order to which, when his arduous work is done, he returns. The high note is heard at once against the ground-bass of the deadliest vice:

Lorsque par un décret des puissances suprêmes,
Le Poète apparaît en ce monde *ennuyé* . . .

31

The romantic cliché of the poet's fate, misunderstood and victimized in an indifferent society, is developed with unexampled ferocity; though, characteristically, it is the intimate hostilities that are emphasized. The mother's lamentations at having given birth to a poet are almost as harsh as the threats of his harpy-fingered wife. The rhythmic vituperation rises to a stridency that verges on the melodramatic but to evaporate in the notably fine stanzas of the close. Redemption through suffering, the price of ransom, is, however precarious its credal foundations, a note struck never more impressively than when, as here, hope can dictate chords of such clear perfection as to dissolve the orchestrated din of mockeries and aspersions. The poem is not a masterpiece; it strains one's suspension of disbelief more, I think, in its virulent denunciations than in its soaring finale. But it exhibits at once that incomparable upward swing from the stasis of ennui and wallowing realism, which reminds us of Anatole France's warning that Baudelaire cannot be regarded simply as the poet of vice.

Most of the pieces in this subsection symbolize the spiritual task of the artist. In *Les Phares* the theme is illustrated from the work of great painters who, like beacons aflame on citadels, pass on the cry of humanity.

The light five-stanzaed *Élévation* which followed *Bénédiction* in the first edition sings of the joyous ascension of the spirit uninhibited by notions of retribution or reward, with a purity of timbre we should not miss in Baudelaire's orchestration. Its implication of intuition into the language of flowers and mute things leads by clear design to the sonnet, *Correspondances*. Upon this, one of the most influential poems of the nineteenth century, ceaseless commentary has fastened since the day when in 1891 the Greek-born Jean Moréas announced that, having meditated on its significance, he had decided that the new school of Decadents should be rechristened 'Symbolists'. Itself a fascinating meditation in fourteen lines rather than a perfect sonnet, this compact repository of mystical reveries, analogies and synaesthesia concentrates a considerable number of ingredients in Baudelaire's thought. Here (to use a favourite image of his) many influences are condensed as in a phial of perfumes, whence they spread out again with effects covering the whole field of modern poetry.

Comme de longs échos qui de loin se confondent
Dans une ténébreuse et profonde unité,
Vaste comme la nuit et comme la clarté,
Les parfums, les couleurs et les sons se répondent.

The Swedenborgian title must not deceive us into holding the
Northern sage wholly or directly responsible for the inspiration
of the poem. Verbally it is composed of reminiscences, largely
unconscious no doubt, of contemporaries and immediate predecessors who were more or less in the stream of Swedenborg's
influence, all of whom however tended to give his doctrine an
interpretation, a transposition in terms of art, which is entirely
their own. Much of the imagery is taken over from Chateaubriand, Balzac and Gérard de Nerval, and their contributions
are combined with examples of synaesthesia from Hoffmann.
The compound that emerges from the crucible has been called a
veritable 'catéchisme de haute esthétique'[1]. As a sonnet it is top-
heavy. A density of suggestion is compressed within the first
quatrain which might have been sufficient alone to launch the
Symbolist movement.

La Nature est un temple où de vivants piliers
Laissent parfois sortir de confuses paroles;
L'homme y passe à travers des forêts de symboles
Qui l'observent avec des regards familiers.

When from what Crépet calls 'the gnomic splendour of these
imperishable formulae' the poet turns to interrogate his own
experience and achievement, Icarus loses his footing in the
clouds and plunges into depths of despondency and despair. His
first reaction is one of quiet self-reproach, *La Muse Malade*, or of
self-raillery, *La Muse Vénale*, producing restrained, familiar and
often perfect verses in a minor key. A more forceful mood of self-
incrimination, *Le Mauvais Moine*, realizes the tragic contrast
between those monks who celebrated their God artistically on
the walls of their cells and the 'mauvais cénobite', who has left
nothing to embellish his odious cloister. 'O moine fainéant!'–the

---

[1] The phrase is Baudelaire's, but is used thus by M Jean Pommier in his enquiry into
the sources and meaning of the sonnet in *La Mystique de Baudelaire*.

burden of self-reproach is too well known to require quoting.
With this sonnet and the next, in which the theme of remorse for
procrastination breaks in upon a retrospective mood to triumph
tragically over the wistful hope of regenerative achievement, we
reach some of the most distinctive poems of the collection:

> Ma jeunesse ne fut qu'un ténébreux orage,
> Traversé çà et là par de brillants soleils;
> Le tonnerre et la pluie ont fait un tel ravage
> Qu'il reste en mon jardin bien peu de fruits vermeils.
>
> Voilà que j'ai touché l'automne des idées;
> Et qu'il faut employer la pelle et les râteaux
> Pour rassembler à neuf les terres inondées,
> Où l'eau creuse des trous grands comme des tombeaux.
>
> Et qui sait si les fleurs nouvelles que je rêve
> Trouveront dans ce sol lavé comme une grève
> Le mystique aliment qui ferait leur vigueur?
>
> – Ô douleur! ô douleur! Le Temps mange la vie,
> Et l'obscur Ennemi qui nous ronge le cœur
> Du sang que nous perdons croît et se fortifie!

The sonnet, *La Beauté*, one of the most frequently quoted but
one of the less original pieces in the collection, introduces new
considerations. Its inspiration is the ideal realized by the plastic
arts of antiquity as interpreted originally by Winckelmann and
shared round by Baudelaire's contemporaries at the instigation
of Leconte de Lisle. For the Parnassians the *beau idéal* was a kind
of divinity, materially embodied in the sculpture of Greece,
whom they worshipped with a fervour derived in part no doubt
from one of those curious diversions of religious feeling characteristic of so many poets and artists in France after 1850. The
reigning goddess was the Venus de Milo (discovered in 1820) and
resemblances exist between Leconte de Lisle's stanzas to her
beauty in the *Poèmes Antiques* of 1852 and Baudelaire's sonnet of
1857. But with one unexpected difference: the palm for impas-
sivity goes this time to Baudelaire.

Originality is more flagrantly achieved in another sonnet, *La*

34

Géante. Here the author's plethoric sensuality is powerfully symbolized in the huge female figure which, lying across the countryside seems, under the spell of the long rhythms which trace her outlines, to become the ample nonchalant naked Earth herself and to prefigure the lure to which the poet will succumb in body and spirit: the obverse of his mystical aspirations and their contamination.

Unlike Leconte de Lisle Baudelaire has no statuesque fixation. Soon he is crying out against the abuse of 'that frightful word, "plastic"', which makes his flesh creep; nor do themes of abstract beauty satisfy him for long. Two pieces seem arranged to cut through this pictorialism with a singular blend of novelty and premonition. Exotic odours emanating from the hair and person of his mulatto mistress excite that olfactory sensitiveness from which he drew some of his most typical effects and, as he unwinds the dark tresses, a flood of nostalgic images reminiscent of his voyage to Mauritius invades the undulations of his five-line stanzas, swelling their sequence into the languorous incantations of *La Chevelure:*

> Longtemps! toujours! ma main dans ta crinière lourde
> Sèmera le rubis, la perle et le saphir,
> Afin qu'à mon désir tu ne sois jamais sourde!
> N'es-tu pas l'oasis où je rêve, et la gourde
> Où je hume à longs traits le vin du souvenir?

But now he is caught in the toils and dives into a vortex of depravity.

> Je t' adore à l'égal de la voûte nocturne,
> O vase de tristesse, ô grande taciturne . . .

The standards of height and depth are precipitously reversed. Adoration drops in ten lines to the level of debauchery. One is tempted to ask if ever the theme of prostitution was treated so flagrantly by a major poet and whether the result is not gross sensationalism? 'The aesthetic love of woman', says M Massin, 'slips insensibly and ever more rapidly towards a sensual frenzy never satisfied, as is witnessed in *Sed non satiata*'. For Mr Eliot, 'His prostitutes, mulattoes, Jewesses, serpents, cats, corpses form

35

a machinery which has not worn very well.' Yet Mr Eliot can agree with Paul Valéry that *Le Balcon*, that perfectly modulated invocation to the 'maîtresse des maîtresses' (the ineluctable mulatto) is one of the most beautiful of Baudelaire's poems. For, and here the characteristic ambivalence reasserts itself, the pieces inspired by Jeanne Duval are not mere exhibitions of corruption; still less are they crude records of debauchery. They are involved in a metaphysique of the conscience–eddies in the vortex of an *âme en peine* round which the series whirls, from which it rebounds and into which it plunges again. The late poem, *Madrigal Triste*, as lovely as *Le Balcon* in its first part, but strangely disturbing in the sequel, was also inspired by Jeanne:

> Je sais que ton cœur, qui regorge
> De vieux amours déracinés,
> Flamboie encor comme une forge,
> Et que tu couves sous ta gorge
> Un peu de l'orgueil des damnés;
>
> Mais tant, ma chère, que tes rêves
> N'auront pas reflété l'Enfer,
> Et qu'en un cauchemar sans trêves,
> Songeant de poisons et de glaives,
> Éprise de poudre et de fer,
>
> N'ouvrant à chacun qu'avec crainte,
> Déchiffrant le malheur partout,
> Te convulsant quand l'heure tinte,
> Tu n'auras pas senti l'étreinte
> De l'irrésistible Dégoût,
>
> Tu ne pourras, esclave reine
> Qui ne m'aimes qu'avec effroi,
> Dans l'horreur de la nuit malsaine
> Me dire, l'âme de cris pleine:
> 'Je suis ton égale, ô mon Roi!'

Distraught power, a desperate sincerity and an impulse of provocation went into the making of many of these pieces, the more interesting of which escape crudity through the intimations they give of a mind at work in reactions of abhorrence and misery–but a mind in fundamental error. The inescapable fury of animal desire is not merely an outrage committed on the flesh; the intimacy is damned in its inception and the pleasure of union is derived from the conviction of its iniquity: 'l'homme et la femme savent que c'est dans la certitude du mal que gît toute volupté'. At times it would seem as if the sexual relationship was conceived as *the* original sin, redeemed, if at all, by the law of procreation:

> Machine aveugle et sourde, en cruautés féconde!
> Salutaire instrument, buveur du sang du monde,
> Comment n'as-tu pas honte et comment n'as-tu pas
> Devant tous les miroirs vu pâlir tes appas?
> La grandeur de ce mal où tu te crois savante
> Ne t'a donc jamais fait reculer d'épouvante,
> Quand la nature, grande en ses desseins cachés,
> De toi se sert, ô femme, ô reine des péchés,
> – De toi, vil animal – pour pétrir un génie?
>
> O fangeuse grandeur! sublime ignominie!

The elevated diction remains a *grand style*, scorched with quasi-biblical imprecations; the long rhythms with their original resources are now devoted to the poetic redemption of the most corrupted of human intimacies. Never since Villon had a major French poet declared so emphatically that the wages of sin is the putrescence of wasted flesh and carious bone. And the question, as I have suggested, is not whether the lesson is driven home with sufficiently revolting detail–few things in literature can equal that notorious *tour de force, La Charogne,*–but whether the antithesis is not at times so abruptly juxtaposed that the mind of the common reader registers *truquage*–shock for shock's sake– even when he may notice the moral so many offended critics seem to have missed?

> – Et pourtant vous serez semblable à cette ordure,
>   A cette horrible infection,
> Étoile de mes yeux, soleil de ma nature
>   Vous, mon ange et ma passion!

Prostitutes, mulattoes, Jewesses, serpents, cats, corpses, vampires, charnel-houses and rainbow-tinted refuse–as Signor Mario Praz has said, the shapeless *putridero* is galvanized into life by Baudelaire, for whom, we may add, the gruesome display is not an end in itself but the trappings of a soul miming its tragedy on the trestle-stage of *bas-romantisme*. This scandalizing, malodorous side of the *Fleurs du Mal* has until recently tended to obsess foreign readers. For too many of us Baudelaire is still the vaguely sinister 'Brother' of Swinburne's *Ave Atque Vale*, though Swinburne had disowned the relationship long before he died.

Considered together the pieces inspired by the Black Venus make a remarkable group. Baudelaire's introspection is a lucid, not a saving grace. But the vitality of his treatment has extracted an astonishing variety of moods out of the liaison and has transmuted them, through the expert manipulation of complex resources, into a set of love poems as distinctive as if they had been written before Romanticism had begun to abuse the theme of the *femme fatale*. Several years ago in the only serious article in English on the art of Baudelaire, Mr Middleton Murry discussed those metallic effects which Leconte de Lisle had commended earlier still. Never were they realized more strikingly than in this vision of frigid womanhood burning with a gemlike flame:

> Ses yeux polis sont faits de minéraux charmants,
> Et dans cette nature étrange et symbolique
> Où l'ange inviolé se mêle au sphinx antique,
> Où tout n'est qu'or, acier, lumière et diamants,
> Resplendit à jamais, comme un astre inutile,
> La froide majesté de la femme stérile.

With the dalliance on the balcony and its euphonious recurrences (the perfect example of the reversible stanza used for incantatory purposes), the tension slackens, the turgid profanity clears and the pure sense of luxury dictates a miniature of perfect charm and grace like *Le Cadre:*

> Comme un beau cadre ajoute à la peinture,
> Bien qu'elle soit d'un pinceau très-vanté,
> Je ne sais quoi d'étrange et d'enchanté
> En l'isolant de l'immense nature,

38

Ainsi bijoux, meubles, métaux, dorure,
S'adaptaient juste à sa rare beauté;
Rien n'offusquait sa parfaite clarté,
Et tout semblait lui servir de bordure.

Même on eût dit parfois qu'elle croyait
Que tout voulait l'aimer; elle noyait
Sa nudité voluptueusement

Dans les baisers du satin et du linge,
Et, lente ou brusque, à chaque mouvement,
Montrait la grâce enfantine du singe.

Semper Eadem, another fine sonnet, introduces a transition so subtly managed that we might be deceived into thinking that between the original protagonists there has been a change of heart. It is not, however, the 'belle ténébreuse' but the radiant blonde who is speaking and to whom the poet replies. He is swept into the circle of her admirers. All but one of the pieces she inspired are presentable. The strong dose of angelicism which etherialises them:

Je suis l'Ange gardien, la Muse et la Madone!

creates an aura similar to that which Edgar Allan Poe contrived whenever he worshipped a woman in verse. One sonnet in the cycle of the White Venus was admittedly prompted by Poe's example. *Le Flambeau Vivant* is composed of a sequence of images adapted from the longer of the poems to Helen, one of the weakest Poe wrote. Sainte-Beuve reproached Baudelaire for 'pétrarquisant sur l'horrible'. How much better than to *pétrarquiser à l'Américaine* when, had he known it, Maurice Scève could have set him an example *beaucoup plus exquis:*

Comme des raiz du Soleil gracieux
Se paissent fleurs durant la Primevere,
Je me recrée aux rayons de ses yeulx,
Et loing, & près autour d'eulx persevere . . .

Apart from the striking line or stanza one comes to expect:

Dans la brute assoupie un ange se réveille,

this group is less original and shows a less effective use of repetitive forms. The piece, *Réversibilité*, is more interesting for its title, a reminiscence of Joseph de Maistre affixed after the verses were sent to Mme Sabatier, than for the enumeration of virtues in the reversible type of stanza. The over-anthologized *Harmonie du Soir* is an automatic pastiche: good lines packed into the form of a Pantoum for a *billet doux*.

It is true of this poet as of the alchemist of whom he says:

Le savant qui lui fait de l'or n'a jamais pu
De son être extirper l'élément corrompu.

When in the somewhat colourless sequence born of the blend of Mme Sabatier's contours and condescensions with the angelicism of Edgar Allan Poe, a drop of venom sharpens the contrasts, then a truly Baudelairian poem is produced. Let us revert to *Semper Eadem* and note the poet's reaction to what Crépet has called the lady's 'chronic joy':

'D'où vous vient, disiez-vous, cette tristesse étrange,
Montant comme la mer sur le roc noir et nu?'
– Quand notre cœur a fait une fois sa vendange,
Vivre est un mal! C'est un secret de tous connu,

Une douleur très simple et non mystérieuse,
Et, comme votre joie, éclatante pour tous.
Cessez donc de chercher, ô belle curieuse!
Et, bien que votre voix soit douce, taisez-vous!

Taisez-vous, ignorante! âme toujours ravie!
Bouche au rire enfantin! Plus encor que la Vie,
La Mort nous tient souvent par des liens subtils.

Laissez, laissez mon cœur s'enivrer d'un *mensonge*,
Plonger dans vos beaux yeux comme dans un beau songe,
Et sommeiller longtemps à l'ombre de vos cils!

Here the attitude is restrained. It becomes positively vicious in another piece which we should have to rescue from the half-dozen condemned, the only one of this series to have been evicted from the original canon. The ineradicable morbidity of the poet's feeling makes him envious of the woman's exuberance; his sadistic spleen flows into a skilful little poem of the most unpleasant perfection, *A Celle qui est trop gaie*, which Sainte-Beuve compared to a masterpiece of Silver Latin.

The nature of the relationship with Mme Sabatier remains conjectural. 'You are for me not only the most attractive of women, of all women, but even more the dearest and most precious of superstitions'. So wrote the poet to her in a very singular letter which Crépet describes as 'd'une rouerie diabolique ou plutôt d'une sincérité désarmée'. It was accompanied by the *Hymne*,

> A la très-chère, à la très-belle
> Qui remplit mon cœur de clarté,
> A l'ange, à l'idole immortelle,
> Salut en l'immortalité!

to save which from destruction George Moore appears to have offered in a magnanimous gesture all the first-born of Europe.

The affair provided occasion for pursuing an ideal of purity, an imaginative opportunity to forget a type of relationship which had so far left little but the taste of depravity and bitter resentment. Whether we think of Baudelaire as a great love poet or not, few poets of the romantic generations have played so many variations on the theme of love sacred and profane. 'To my mind,' said Verlaine, 'the originality of Charles Baudelaire is to represent powerfully and essentially modern man on the physical plane ('l'homme physique moderne'), such as the refinements of an excessive civilization have made him'. A limited view, but perhaps worth recording.

The 'white' cycle dissolves imperceptibly into a further series which Crépet suggests calling the cycle of the 'femme aux yeux verts'. It was inspired by an actress whose hair was golden and whose eyes were green, but whose complete identity has not emerged until recently. We have already referred to Marie Daubrun. One of the loveliest lyrics in the French language, the faultless *Invitation au Voyage*, unique in its fluid combination of

41

five and seven syllables, the prototype of Verlaine's 'Impair', was inspired by her beauty. The turbid vision has completely cleared; the sensual fever has cooled into a fervent *amitié*. One does not feel the person imposing her presence, obsessing the poem; she is exquisitely distanced, blended into a scene, lightly evoked, which is her 'correspondance'. We see how effectively, though at a great remove, the Doctrine could be transmuted. Again for a moment the supernatural interest has captured the poet's imagination and transformed existence:

> Là, tout n'est qu'ordre et beauté,
> Luxe, calme et volupté.

'Alas!' said Théodore de Banville commenting on this poem 'Who can fail to see? The lovers will never set out and the country where all is order and beauty would be too perfect ever to be inhabited by figures of mortality'. Banville knew; it was he, not Baudelaire, who made the 'voyage amoureux' with Marie Daubrun.

Of all his associations this seems to have been the most beneficent to the poet. To *L'Invitation* some critics seem to prefer the equally perfect, though even less personal, *Chant d'Automne:*

> J'aime de vos longs yeux la lumière verdâtre
> Douce beauté, mais tout aujourd'hui m'est amer . . .

But while the pieces known to have been inspired by Marie are free from dross, they are not all euphoric. *L'Irréparable* is one of the most disquieting of the collection. According to Crépet this mysterious and powerful poem is built up of two elements: the conviction of the irremissible felt by a soul smitten with remorse and a set of images and formulae precisely related to a play of which Marie was the principal interpreter. The perfect fusion of these images used as symbols with the favourite reversible form produces a strange fascination. The piece has an envoy. An apparition in gauze and gold illuminates the depth of a banal theatre, reminding one of a scene Sickert was fond of painting. But stanzas like the following have the more haunting, if sinister, effect:

> L'Espérance qui brille aux carreaux de l'Auberge
> Est soufflée, est morte à jamais!
> Sans lune et sans rayons, trouver où l'on héberge
> Les martyrs d'un chemin mauvais!
> Le Diable a tout éteint aux carreaux de l'Auberge!

The series ends in despondency. The Ideal withdraws, while Spleen progressively invades all avenues and contaminates all feelings. It is remarkable how much interest romanticism has extracted from the analysis of ennui; and even more remarkable that Baudelaire could have extended the field of morbid interest so as to make it almost his own. The gravity he attaches to the deeper depressions of the spirit has already been noted. What appears from these final pieces is the variety of treatment applied to *tædium vitae* experienced in its many forms: moral paralysis, reaction from excesses, claustrophobia of the void which is a cell, a vault, the dropped lid of asphyxiation, the weight of dead bodies on wounded limbs; or again that *goût du néant* the poet shared with his contemporaries, and all the vagaries of boredom, rainy days, mists, snowflakes and thunder showers which will become favourite motifs with so many of his successors, whose fragile, ephemeral impressionism has made us forget that most of what was worth saying about such moods had been exploited two or three decades earlier, with a charm and subtlety of which this rough enumeration can have given no idea:

> Le Printemps adorable a perdu son odeur . . .

if with a certain formal monotony from which relief is rare:

> La musique souvent me prend comme une mer!
> Vers ma pâle étoile,
> Sous un plafond de brume ou dans un vaste éther,
> Je mets à la voile . . .

As with all French poetry of the mid-nineteenth century–apart from the persistent virtuosity with which Hugo in exile challenged Ronsard–line and stanza are insufficiently varied to satisfy our restless taste for protean forms. But the alexandrine is so magnificently handled in overtures and passages of almost disproportionate amplitude and force, that no other poet since Racine has given a more impressive exhibition of its finer uses. Indeed its exploitation for effects of power and solemnity by masters like Baudelaire and Leconte de Lisle may have exhausted its potency for a time by discouraging further experiment; and this may help to explain the subsequent deviation to freer modes and even the flight to apparent formlessness.

The last few poems of this series escape these reservations. The two pieces in octosyllabic quatrains, *L'Héautontimorouménos* and *L'Irrémédiable* revert to the more sinister vein. Both are related to ideas formulated by Joseph de Maistre; but they have so deep a hinterland and convey implications so obscure that expert commentators like M Crépet and M Blin should be consulted for enlightenment. May it suffice here to say that these pieces reflect the most intense preoccupation with their author's sombre predicament. The first revolves round the idea that the sinner torments himself in tormenting others:

> Ne suis-je pas un faux accord
> Dans la divine symphonie,
> Grâce à la vorace Ironie
> Qui me secoue et qui me mord?
>
> Elle est dans ma voix, la criarde!
> C'est tout mon sang, ce poison noir!
> Je suis le sinistre miroir
> Où la mégère se regarde.
>
> Je suis la plaie et le couteau!
> Je suis le soufflet et la joue!
> Je suis les membres et la roue,
> Et la victime et le bourreau!

In the second the images illustrate the irremediable plight of the erring soul ensnared into ironic dialogue with itself, having realized that it cannot escape its predicament of being irrevocably 'blocked in the consciousness of evil' (Crépet). What is remarkable here is that the terrible insight, as it probes the pit of introspection, arms itself with a type of imagery few modern poets have had the courage to use for interrogating the motives of iniquity and raising the confession to the level of a 'dark and splendid' lyricism.

> Un Ange, imprudent voyageur
> Qu'a tenté l'amour du difforme,
> Au fond d'un cauchemar énorme
> Se débattant comme un nageur,
>
> Et luttant, angoisses funèbres!
> Contre un gigantesque remous
> Qui va chantant comme les fous
> Et pirouettant dans les ténèbres . . .
>
> Un damné descendant sans lampe,
> Au bord d'un gouffre dont l'odeur
> Trahit l'humide profondeur,
> D'éternels escaliers sans rampe,
>
> Où veillent des monstres visqueux
> Dont les larges yeux de phosphore
> Font une nuit plus noire encore
> Et ne rendent visibles qu'eux; . . .

In such pieces as these, if nowhere else, Baudelaire seems to have won his unique and perilous wager to extract beauty from evil.

*

Considering the notorious sensitiveness of Second Empire censorship, it is surprising to find how few of the *fleurs maladives* were condemned. For the man the judgment was a severe blow; for the poet it was a spur. Soon he was writing to tell Hugo that he had produced three times as many poems as had been suppressed.

The series of about twenty that compose the *Tableaux Parisiens* are very unequal in value. The uninitiated should not be put off by the first two or identify the climax with the last of all—pedestrian pieces of moralizing, in the manner of Sainte-Beuve, amongst the earliest of those collected and obviously immature. They do however contribute to the greater objectivity of this phase; and many in the subsequent sections could find their place under the same rubric. The three central poems show an acute sense of types of personal tragedy involved in the social order. Baudelaire was not even a 'Socialiste mitigé' (a phrase scribbled against a stanza which he suppressed). What criticism of society he indulges in shows a sense of wrongs more deeply interfused than social injustices. It is not the social or even the moral order that is wrong but the vindictiveness of the mysterious order of the universe–and this order is not branded as Satanic. The pariahs of society and the pariah poet himself are the victims, not of God's vengeance, but of his inscrutable law. From the pathos of his own plight Baudelaire reacts in a superb effort of compassion: he is the founder of the modern order of pariah poets, the order that feeds on destitution to-day.

Le Cygne is a poem of exile. Formally it is perhaps the most original piece in the collection, combining a number of classical, romantic and modern themes in a quasi-symphonic arrangement. Though some commentators ignore the musical character of the composition, this aspect seems inescapable, based as it is on an expert use of recurrent motifs, not regularly disposed, their discords of tempo, tone and imagery resolving into the harmonies and psychological unity of a new kind of incantatory poem, a prototype for much Symbolist experimentation. The first phrase, 'Andromaque, je pense à vous!' gives the musical lead. Developed in the opening stanza with a rhythmic majesty which recalls Racine, it is presented as a memory occurring to the poet as he crosses the Place du Carrousel, then in process of being cleared. Here a break occurs in the middle of a quatrain and the second theme arrives, a topographical aside made in colloquial tones:

> Le vieux Paris n'est plus (la forme d'une ville
> Change plus vite, hélas! que le cœur d'un mortel).

As he evokes the former scene a new memory supervenes, that of a menagerie from which a swan had escaped to search for water in the dusty soil. The unhappy bird appeals in vain to heaven, 'comme l'homme d'Ovide', a reminiscence which is not developed but lends support to the main subject.

The poem is arranged in two movements. The second picks up the theme of Paris through whose contemporary transformation the earlier scene re-emerges. The incidents are distanced and recur, as it were, in the depths of reverie or meditation, bringing back first the thought of the swan with its mad gestures of unquenchable desire and then, in a magnificent stanza:

> Andromaque, des bras d'un grand époux tombée,
> Vil bétail, sous la main du superbe Pyrrhus,
> Auprès d'un tombeau vide en extase courbée;
> Veuve d'Hector, hélas! et femme d'Hélénus!

And now a *séquelle* of lesser exiles, beginning significantly with,

> Je pense à la négresse, amaigrie et phtisique . . .

broadens into an 'anaphoric enumeration' of the lost, the abandoned, the bereft, the orphaned, and the poem fades effectively into an unusually casual echo. Throughout, the characteristic sense of nostalgia diffuses a vague poignancy over its finely modulated moods, ranging from those inspired by commonplaces of human and animal deprivation to the heights of legendary misfortune. Its controlled melancholy, muted sympathy and effortless variations have made this piece a supreme favourite with many critics.

The three poems, *Le Cygne, Les Sept Vieillards, Les Petites Vieilles*, are each dedicated to Victor Hugo and owe a degree of their impulsion to his example. It would be unfair to compare with its counterpart avowed or suspected in the elder poet's work, any of Baudelaire's masterpieces. An abyss separates the technical brilliance of *Les Orientales* (one of which was the prototype of *Les Sept Vieillards*) from the maturity of an art of imaginative compassion rigorously controlled by irony and by a kind of astringent malice displayed in a poem written, as Baudelaire admitted to Hugo, '*in view of imitating you* (laugh with me at my fatuity), after having re-read a few of your collected pieces in which a magnificent charity mingles with a touching familiarity'. In Hugo we find a genuine warmth of sympathy, at times broadly humanitarian, often topically particularized, flowing into verses so unequal in power that the 'pitié suprême' can become commonplace in sweep and insensitive in detail. *Océano Nox* is by no means an insignificant example, but we know with what prodigious irony Tristan Corbière rewrote it. The trenchant, racy colloquialism of Corbière's manner is not Baudelaire's forte, though there are familiar touches in many of his poems which add to their effect. Much more characteristic is the control of powerful feelings–the exile's nostalgia distanced and allegorized in the first, the convulsive compassion that seems to deny itself direct outlet in the third and which throbs under a curb of malignity behind the phantasmagoria of the Seven Old Men.

A number of gratuitous *précisions* have been offered by commentators in their efforts to find sources of suggestion for this weird creation. It would hardly be more extraneous to recall the role of the Brocken spectre in German and English romantic literature. A certain conjugation of sunlight and mist was capable of projecting the amplified silhouette of a spectator standing against its luminous haze. The poets were impressed and drew marvels and morals from meditating on this phenomenon. In Baudelaire's poem hallucinatory deformation of another kind is used with consummate skill as if to evoke in one condensed human impression that sense of horror and absurdity in the universe which Hugo's vision tended to magnify. The poet is returning at daybreak along a street in Paris, thick with fog drifting like a river between the banks of high facades. The fog parts and a frightfully vindictive figure appears and disappears. Seven times like Banquo's ghost the apparition strikes its hideous reiterations into the poet's brain until,

> Exaspéré comme un ivrogne qui voit double,
> Je rentrai, je fermai ma porte, épouvanté,
> Malade et morfondu, l'esprit fiévreux et trouble,
> Blessé par le mystère et par l'absurdité!

It was when acknowledging these 'vers saisissants' that Hugo wrote the famous phrase: 'Vous dotez le ciel de l'art d'on ne sait quel rayon macabre. Vous créez un frisson nouveau'.

Les Petites Vieilles is a more human and detailed study of the pathos of destitution. Its length precludes treatment here. Of one *laisse* of quatrains which gives the sense of the whole, Marcel Proust wrote 'il semble impossible d'aller plus loin'.

Ah! que j'en ai suivi, de ces petites vieilles!
Une, entre autres, à l'heure où le soleil tombant
Ensanglante le ciel de blessures vermeilles,
Pensive, s'asseyait à l'écart sur un banc,

Pour entendre un de ces concerts, riches de cuivre,
Dont les soldats parfois inondent nos jardins,
Et qui, dans ces soirs d'or où l'on se sent revivre,
Versent quelque héroïsme au cœur des citadins.

Celle-là, droite encor, fière et sentant la règle,
Humait avidement ce chant vif et guerrier;
Son œil parfois s'ouvrait comme l'œil d'un vieil aigle;
Son front de marbre avait l'air fait pour le laurier!

Several other pieces, lesser in scope but of equal poignancy,
support the central triptych. Among the rest a few have the chill
air of eighteenth-century secular homilies; but there are one or
two modest gems in which the warmth of intimacy is felt. The
simple impression which begins

Je n'ai pas oublié, voisine de la ville,
Notre blanche maison, petite mais tranquille . . .

is obviously the model of that touching sonnet of Verlaine's
Après Trois Ans; it seems to forecast his brief reveries on the
prospect of happy domesticity, the reality of which was shattered
by the ruffianly intrusion of Rimbaud. When however we turn
to Baudelaire's moving lines to the memory of his old nurse we
are struck with a type of sentiment which might suggest comparison with that late masterpiece of Flaubert, *Un Cœur Simple:*

La servante au grand cœur dont vous étiez jalouse,
Et qui dort son sommeil sous une humble pelouse,
Nous devrions pourtant lui porter quelques fleurs . . .

But the meditation develops against a background of eternity
with a sweep of vision neither Flaubert nor Verlaine could have
approached. If it were necessary to show how effectively in a few
lines Baudelaire could handle profound but simple feeling, one

would point to this little poem, surely a masterpiece of natural pathos:

> Lorsque la bûche siffle et chante, si le soir,
> Calme, dans le fauteuil je la voyais s'asseoir,
> Si, par une nuit bleue et froide de décembre,
> Je la trouvais tapie en un coin de ma chambre,
> Grave, et venant du fond de son lit éternel
> Couver l'enfant grandi de son œil maternel,
> Que pourrais-je répondre à cette âme pieuse,
> Voyant tomber des pleurs de sa paupière creuse?

*

The concluding subdivisions are short. Less than thirty poems are distributed under the rubrics, *Le Vin, Fleurs du Mal, Révolte, La Mort*. But they contain some significant additions to the presentation of the poet's philosophy interspersed with a few of the most perfect examples of his art. The use of the general title for the second of these parts indicates a concentration of interest on what Crépet calls the cycle of vice, 'du vice clairvoyant, du vice désespéré, du vice puni'[1] Not that there is mere repetition: a variety of vices are analysed with a daring which incurred excision and resulted in a redistribution of contents. Reset in their original order this series would be worth the special attention, not of a superficial moralist whose conclusion could be anticipated, but of the ideal critic armed with psychological, theological and above all literary acumen. For here we have something of a very different order from the charnel-house paraphernalia which clogs access to the essential laboratory from whose crucibles and alembics the Baudelairian toxins are distilled into phials of exquisite shape and colour. Were that critic at hand, having elicited his views on the depth and courage of the 'dolorous programme' attempted in these pieces, I should like to suggest to him that this section reveals, along with the temerity, the *limits* of Baudelaire's genius: it delimits his actual achievement as that of a major, not a great, poet. For all his fascination with human error, the range of evils analysed in his work is narrow: they are predominantly, though not exclusively, sexual.

[1] The phrase is Thibaudet's.

◁

And they are regarded as *secret* sins, sins against the self or against God, not as sins against society. Even when they are felt to be sins against the *other*, they are still not envisaged as sins against society. Adultery, the social form of sexual transgression, the *péché mignon* of the French literary tradition from the Arthurian romances to the great series of psychological studies ending with *Madame Bovary*, is of no interest to Baudelaire. In this alone his inferiority to Racine is such as to differentiate him as a great introspective from a great dramatist and, for all the maturity he demands of his readers, to prompt the question whether he himself had time to survive his 'stormy' adolescence?

But whatever else they reveal or lack, few of these pieces fail to bear witness to that vigilance of the judgment already differentiated. Indeed the most celebrated poem in this group, *Un Voyage à Cythère*, is at once the most brilliant and the most realistic sermon in verse he ever extemporized on the text, 'The wages of sin is death'–if one can use the word 'extemporized' of a theme he returned to so often. Explicitly a symbol, and the most brutal of moral lessons read to himself and to the erring generations of romanticism, this poem was greatly admired by Flaubert who may have seen in it, condensed beyond his powers of concentration, the lesson he made implicit in *Madame Bovary*.

Révolte comprises three short pieces which might, for the little they add to the total effect, have been distributed among the rest. Presumably intended to mark an essential attitude, they lack the strength to demonstrate it distinctively as compared with its expression elsewhere in the collection. The first, in which God is conceived as a tyrant, indifferent to the torments of the martyred, is addressed to the supreme Martyr who is reminded of the successful days of his mission and of the desertion he suffered at the end. Did Christ feel remorse? As for the poet–the last stanza is worth quoting if only for its second line:

> – Certes, je sortirai, quant à moi, satisfait
> D'un monde où l'action n'est pas la sœur du rêve;
> Puissé-je user du glaive et périr par le glaive!
> Saint Pierre a renié Jésus . . . il a bien fait!

Mme Aupick protested against the inclusion of this early piece (known to have existed in 1847) in the 1868 edition of her son's poems, asserting that 'he would not have written it later, since he had been in sympathy with religion for some years'. Only a threat to abandon the editorial project could scare her into submission. Of more interest is the fact that, when the piece had appeared in 1857, it was preceded by a foreword probably intended to defend the author from a charge of blasphemy. One sentence throws a useful light on his attitude to the task in hand: 'Fidèle à son douloureux programme, l'auteur des *Fleurs du Mal* a dû en parfait comédien façonner son esprit à tous les sophismes comme à toutes les corruptions.'

Les Litanies de Satan were selected by Swinburne for special praise. They are a version, showing some slight novelty of form, of the romantic apotheosis of the Devil as patron saint of exiles and outcasts. Though the language is not free from clichés, nothing Baudelaire wrote could lack originality of phrase. The personification of hope as 'une fille charmante' made his mother forgive him the poem and later won the admiration of Mallarmé. In summing up reminiscences and borrowings Crépet drops the hint that there are more texts which denounce the presence or malice of the Devil than litanies that extol him. One cannot indeed suppress a comparison between what Baudelaire assimilates and what he feels. His romanticized Miltonic Prometheus is a fine enough fiction. The Devil with whom he was familiar he seems to have cared for very much less.

The final section on Death is, if not one of the richest, at least one of the most attractive of the groups. It is composed of five sonnets, simple in structure but of subtle charm, followed by the longest and, many think, the greatest of all Baudelaire's poems. The first sonnet, *La Mort des Amants*, is one of his most perfect trifles–if a thing so perfect can be called a trifle. Worked, as it were, in soft colours on shot silk yet free from languorousness, touched but not steeped in the sheen of luxury, it illustrates the significance of that self-sufficing objective so fondly characterized as writing a poem for the poem's sake. Villiers de l'Isle-Adam thought it a *tour de force* in which Baudelaire had applied his musical theories. Both Villiers and Debussy set the sonnet to music:

Nous aurons des lits pleins d'odeurs légères,
Des divans profonds comme des tombeaux,

Et d'étranges fleurs sur des étagères,
Écloses pour nous sous des cieux plus beaux.

Usant à l'envi leurs chaleurs dernières,
Nos deux cœurs seront deux vastes flambeaux,
Qui réfléchiront leurs doubles lumières
Dans nos deux esprits, ces miroirs jumeaux.

Un soir fait de rose et de bleu mystique,
Nous échangerons un éclair unique,
Comme un long sanglot, tout chargé d'adieux;

Et plus tard un Ange, entr'ouvrant les portes,
Viendra ranimer, fidèle et joyeux,
Les miroirs ternis et les flammes mortes.

The lightness which characterizes these sonnets is not absent from the finale. *Le Voyage* is a poem, not of death, but of departure. Not an escapist poem either, but a piece of inspired meditation on the fatuity of escapism. Anything but a poem written for its own sake, it is full of restrained irony at the illusions of restless *déplacement*. Baudelaire professed a hatred of direct moralizing; but meditation on the fruits of desire and activity is one of the strengths of his collection. *Le Voyage* is a poem which conforms to the definition, a 'criticism of life'.

A noble exhilaration carries the quatrains on with a fine swing of controlled rapture toward the unknown, even if the unknown proves to be

Le spectacle ennuyeux de l'immortel péché.

The famous envoy constitutes a supreme achievement in its fusion of strange serenity of feeling with mastery of the long, nervous, solemn yet exultant rhythm:

O Mort, vieux capitaine, il est temps! levons l'ancre!
Ce pays nous ennuie, ô Mort! Appareillons!
Si le ciel et la mer sont noirs comme de l'encre,
Nos cœurs que tu connais sont remplis de rayons!

Verse-nous ton poison pour qu'il nous réconforte!
Nous voulons, tant ce feu nous brûle le cerveau,
Plonger au fond du gouffre, Enfer ou Ciel, qu'importe?
Au fond de l'Inconnu pour trouver du *nouveau*!

The poet of Death? Not, surely, in the sense Lanson seems to have implied. Baudelaire is not a necrological poet. As Crépet says, he had no wish to close his book on a cry of despair: to die was to escape '*anywhere out of the world*', to fly at full sail towards 'an unknown conceived as a new life!'[1]

*

Few recent editions of Baudelaire's poems are contrived to end with *Le Voyage;* some relegate the condemned pieces to an appendix and most suffix a number unpublished when the poet died, juvenilia or late discoveries, which bring the total of his pieces of verse to nearly two hundred. Many of these additions are inferior; but a few are among the most important of all his poems. Either they attain the aesthetic purity of the famous sonnet, *Recueillement*, or they combine different degrees of such quality with unusual psychological or philosophical significance such as, in different ways, the exquisite, if 'sadistic', *Madrigal Triste*, that Pascalian sonnet, *Le Gouffre*, and above all *L'Imprévu*, uniquely valuable as a reflection of the final state of his mind and art.

If I had to choose one of the two sonnets to quote in conclusion, I should select *Le Gouffre*. *Recueillement* has the advantage of being one of the best known of all French sonnets. It is a faultless specimen (or, if Paul Valéry was right, a flawed masterpiece) of its author's contemplative melancholy expressed through natural symbols (Baudelaire was by no means so indifferent to nature as he professed to be). Its great virtue is its unity of design harmoniously developed through a sequence of personifications. The sestet is 'Miltonic', not traditional in form; the refinement it adds to the romantic treatment of nightfall effaces all precedents.

If *Recueillement* is the last achievement of the pure poet, *Le Gouffre* brings us back to the horrors of an existence approaching the brink of dissolution. In this piece of agitated rhetoric—clearly

[1] *Les Fleurs du Mal* (ed. Corti), p. 265.

reflecting the nightmares of which Baudelaire complained that they were so terrible, he would have preferred not to fall asleep–he seems to hold out one hand to Pascal and the other to Hopkins. For I doubt if this sonnet had any counterpart in nineteenth-century poetry until it was surpassed by Hopkins's 'No worst, there is none':

> O the mind, mind has mountains; cliffs of fall
> Frightful, sheer, no-man-fathomed . . .

For all their diversity Pascal, Baudelaire and Hopkins meet in the depths of the sublime. Mastery of style devoted to sounding the abyss of desolation:

> Pascal avait son gouffre, avec lui se mouvant.
> – Hélas! tout est abîme, – action, désir, rêve,
> Parole! Et sur mon poil qui tout droit se relève
> Mainte fois de la Peur je sens passer le vent.
>
> En haut, en bas, partout, la profondeur, la grève,
> Le silence, l'espace affreux et captivant . . .
> Sur le fond de mes nuits Dieu de son doigt savant
> Dessine un cauchemar multiforme et sans trêve.
>
> J'ai peur du sommeil comme on a peur d'un grand trou,
> Tout plein de vague horreur, menant on ne sait où;
> Je ne vois qu'infini par toutes les fenêtres,
>
> Et mon esprit, toujours du vertige hanté,
> Jalouse du néant l'insensibilité.
> – Ah! ne jamais sortir des Nombres et des Êtres!

L'Imprévu appears to be the last significant poem Baudelaire wrote, and few poems show more clearly how he had matured. Certain characteristic persistences enable one to compare this piece with the first two of the collection. The *Au Lecteur*, read in conjunction with the end of *Bénédiction*, presents the same anti-thesis of degradation and sublimity, of worldly corruption and hypocrisy juxtaposed to supernatural assurance. But a quasi-identity of phrase brings out the contrast. The line:

Car il est fait avec l'universel Péché . . .

should be compared with one of the last lines of *Bénédiction*–and contrasted, for here the Devil is speaking in the role of Mephistopheles (the irony of the poem is in deadly earnest), come to claim his own, those who have profited by their sins. Then the unforeseen happens. An angel 'perched above the universe' clarions the victory of those who have accepted suffering,

> De ceux dont le cœur dit: 'Que béni soit ton fouet,
> Seigneur! que la douleur, ô Père, soit bénie!
> Mon âme dans tes mains n'est pas un vain jouet,
> Et ta prudence est infinie.'

The saving grace of suffering is no longer thought of as that of the vicarious artist: all who suffer earn ransom through submission.

'Ce beau poème', as Crépet is constrained to call it, was written for Barbey d'Aurevilly in response, not merely to the judgment already cited from the close of his famous review, but probably to a more recent parting shot–'Adieu le dernier de mes vices. Quand deviendrez-vous une vertu?' sent in a note dated 8th January 1863. On the 15th of that month *L'Imprévu* appeared in a journal called *Le Boulevard*, accompanied by a couple of editorial notes, undoubtedly by the author of the poem. One explains the use of an indecency. The other may be one of the most significant phrases Baudelaire has left us. We could do no better than take our leave of him by quoting it:

> 'Ici l'auteur des *Fleurs du Mal* se tourne vers la Vie éternelle.
> Ca devait finir comme ça.
> Observons que, comme tous les nouveaux convertis, il se montre très-rigoureux et très-fanatique.'

Supernatural preoccupation, delicate irony, mystery–the best of Baudelaire is there, with the incomparable accent he alone could have characterized, 'l'accent de l'immortalité'.

APPENDIX

Translations of passages quoted in the text

p. 11. I know that you keep a place for the poet in the blessed ranks of the holy Legions and that you invite him to the eternal fête of Thrones, Virtues and Dominions.

I know that suffering is the unique nobility on which neither earth nor hell can make incision and that to weave my mystic crown all ages and all worlds must be put under contribution.

p. 13. Through his wilful and forceful love of the bizarre, but still more by his masterly technique, Baudelaire has exerted considerable influence.

p. 16. I give you these verses so that if my name succeeds in reaching distant ages, to fill men's minds of an evening with dreams, like a ship favoured by a strong north wind, the memory of you will, as wavering fables do, disturb the reader like a dulcimer, suspended by a link, mystic and fraternal, to my superb rhymes.

Accursed being to whom, from the depth of the abyss to the height of heaven, nothing responds save me—oh, you who, like a shadow whose tracks are ephemeral, tread down with light foot and serene glance the stupid mortals who have judged you harshly, statue with eyes of jet, high angel with brow of bronze!

p. 20. Sombre yet limpid tête-à-tête, when a heart becomes its own mirror! Well of truth, clear yet dark, in which a livid star trembles,

An ironic infernal beacon, a torch satanically graceful, comfort and glory unique,—the consciousness of Evil!

p. 21. It was impossible to show otherwise the agitation of the spirit in the toils of sin.

p. 21. 'And you have chosen Hell, you have turned yourself into the Devil . . . in petrarchizing on the horrible you look as if you had been amusing yourself,—yet you must have suffered a great deal, my poor young friend.'

p. 21. It's a cry repeated by a thousand sentinels, an order passed on by a thousand amplifiers, a beacon lit on a thousand citadels, the call of huntsmen lost in the great woods.

For truly, Lord, it is the best witness we could give of our dignity, this ardent sob which rolls from age to age to die at last on the brink of thy eternity!

p. 22. Ruins! my kindred! oh minds cognate with mine! I bid you each night a solemn farewell! Where will you be tomorrow, octogenarian Eves, on whom God's clawed fist falls with frightful weight?

p. 23. Poetry, for him who will descend however little into himself, interrogate his soul and recall his fervent memories, has no other end but itself; it can have no other end, and no poem will be so great, so noble, so truly deserving to be called a poem, as that which will have been written solely for the pleasure of writing a poem.

p. 24. Need I tell you that in this atrocious book I have put all my heart, all my affection, all my religion (disguised), all my hatred? True, I'll write the contrary; I'll swear by the high gods that it's a book of pure art, of mimicry, of charlatanism; and I'll lie outright.

57

p. 24. Romanticism implies modern art, that is intimacy, spirituality, colour, aspiration towards the infinite, expressed by all the means possessed by the arts.

p. 24. Orgy is not the sister of inspiration; we have put an end to that adulterous parentage.

p. 24. Illustrious poets had for long shared between them the most flowery provinces of the poetic domain. It seemed amusing to me, and all the more agreeable because the task was so difficult, to extract beauty from Evil. This book, essentially useless and absolutely innocent, has been writtenf or no other purpose than to amuse me and to exercise my pronounced taste for the obstacle.

p. 25. the desire, in a word, for a more solid content and for a purer form.

p. 25. To ask what they really are will reveal once again, if that is necessary, that they have not proceeded from a meditation on the nature of the literary achievement, but from an experience intense, metaphysical and religious, of which the literary achievement is but the ultimate and intelligent expression, in disguise.

p. 26. I have done my duty like a perfect chemist and like a saint.

p. 26. Poetry is what is most real, what is only completely true in another world. This world is a dictionary of hieroglyphics.

p. 28. It is that wonderful, that immortal instinct for the beautiful which makes us consider the earth and its spectacles as an *aperçu*, a correspondence of Heaven.

p. 28. In the great poets there is no metaphor, comparison or epithet which is not adapted with mathematical exactitude to the particular circumstance, because such comparisons, such metaphors and epithets are drawn from the inexhaustible store of universal analogies, and cannot be drawn from anywhere else.

p. 28. Angels clothed in gold, purple and hyacinth, be ye witnesses that I have done my duty like a perfect chemist and like a saint.

p. 33. Like long echoes which mingle from afar in a dark and profound unity, vast as night and as the light, perfumes, colours and sounds respond to one another.

p. 33. Nature is a temple whose living pillars emit now and then confused words; man passes that way through forests of symbols which watch him with familiar glances.

p. 34. My youth was nothing but a darkling storm, traversed here and there by brilliant sunlight. Thunder and rain have made such havoc that in my garden very few scarlet fruits are left.
    Now I have reached the autumn of ideas; and now rake and shovel must be used to assemble afresh the inundated earth in which water scoops holes as big as graves.
    And who knows if the new flowers of which I dream will find in this soil, washed like a strand, the mystic nourishment to supply their vigour?
    O sorrow! O sorrow! Time eats into life, and the dark Enemy that gnaws at our heart by the blood we lose increases and fortifies himself!

p. 35. For long! for ever! my hand in your heavy mane will sow rubies, pearls and sapphires so that to my desire you will never be deaf! Are you not the oasis where I dream and the gourd in which I drink deep of the wine of memory?

58

p. 35. I adore you as I adore the vault of night, oh vase of sorrow, most taciturn one . . .

p. 36. I know that your heart which brims over with old up-rooted loves still flames like a forge and that in your bosom broods something of the pride of the damned.

But so long, my dear, as your dreams will not have reflected Hell; so long as in an endless nightmare, dreaming of poisons and swords, enamoured of powder and steel,

Opening to each one fearfully, deciphering mishap everywhere, you will not have felt convulsively, when the bell tolls, the clutch of irresistible Disgust,

You will never be able, my slave-queen, who love me only in terror, in the baleful night of horror to tell me in a cry gushing from your soul, 'I am your equal, oh my King!'

p. 37. Man and woman know that all pleasure lies in the certitude of doing wrong.

p. 37. Blind and deaf machine, fertile in cruelties! Salutary instrument, drunk with the blood of the world, have you no shame, have you not seen your charms pale in all mirrors? The extent of this evil in which you think yourself skilled, has it never made you wilt in fright, when nature, great in her hidden designs, makes use of you, oh woman, oh queen of sins,–of you, vile animal–to knead a genius? O filthy grandeur! sublime ignominy!

p. 37. And yet you will be like this filth, this horrible corruption, star of my eyes, sun of my nature, you, my angel, my passion!

p. 38. Her polished eyes are made of charming minerals and in her strange symbolic nature which blends the inviolate angel with the antique sphinx, in which all is gold, steel, light and diamonds, there shines for ever, like a useless star, the cold majesty of the sterile woman.

p. 38. As a fine frame adds to a picture, though painted by a vaunted brush, some mysterious strangeness and enchantment in isolating it from immense nature, so jewels, furniture, metals, gilt adapted themselves precisely to her rare beauty; nothing obscured her perfect brightness and all things seemed to serve her as border. One would even say at times that she believed everything wished to love her; she bathed her nudity voluptuously in kisses of satin and linen and, slow or brisk, each movement showed a monkey's childlike grace.

p. 39. As on rays of the gracious Sun flowers feed during Spring, I renew my life in the beams of her eyes, and far and near persevere in their circuit . . .

p. 40. The learned man who makes him gold has never succeeded in extirpating the element of corruption from his own being.

p. 40. 'Whence comes', you asked, 'this strange sadness, rising like the sea over a bare black rock?'–Once our heart has reaped its harvest, to live on is an evil! It is a secret known to all, a most simple sorrow and not mysterious, and, like your joy, it shines for all to see. Cease then to seek, oh fair inquisitive one! and though your voice is sweet, keep still! Keep still, ignorant one! soul ever ravished with joy! Lips that laugh like a child's! More still than life, Death holds us often by subtle bonds. Let, let my heart drink deep of a *lie*, plunge into your fine eyes as into a fine dream, and slumber long in the shadow of your lashes!

p. 41. . . . of a diabolical knavery or rather a sincerity disarmed.

p. 41. To the most dear, to the most fair who fills my heart with light, to the angel, the idol immortal, salutation in immortality!

59

p. 42. There all is order and beauty, luxury, calm and pleasure.

p. 42. I love of your long glances the greenish light, sweet beauty, but for me today all things are bitter.

p. 43. The Hope which shines in the panes of the Inn is blown out, is dead for ever! Without moon or rays how to find where they shelter the martyrs of an evil road! The Devil has extinguished all light in the panes of the Inn!

p. 43. Music often seizes me like a tide! Towards my pale star, under a ceiling of fog or in a vast expanse of air, I sail out to sea.

p. 44. Am I not a false chord in the divine symphony, thanks to the voracious Irony which shakes and rends me?
It shrieks in my voice! It is all my blood, this black poison! I am the sinister mirror in which the shrew looks at herself.
I am the wound and the knife! I am the blow and the cheek! I am the limbs and the wheel, And the victim and the executioner!

p. 45. An Angel, imprudent traveller, tempted by love of the deformed, in the depths of a huge nightmare, writhing like a swimmer,
And struggling in funereal anguish against a gigantic eddy which goes singing like madmen and wheeling in the darkness . . .
One of the damned descending without a lamp, at the edge of an abyss whose odour betrays the humid depth of eternal staircases without banisters,
Where watch viscous monsters whose wide eyes of phosphorus make a still blacker night and leave only themselves visible . . .

p. 46. Old Paris is no longer (the form of a town changes more quickly alas! than the heart of a mortal).

p. 47. Andromache, from the arms of a great spouse, fallen like a low beast under the hand of proud Pyrrhus, bowing enrapt before an empty tomb, widow of Hector, alas! and wife of Helenus!

p. 48. Exasperated like a drunkard who sees double, I returned home, closed my door, terrified, sick and numb, my mind feverish and confounded, wounded by mystery and absurdity!

p. 48. You endow the heaven of art with an indefinable ray of the macabre. You create a new thrill.

p. 49. Ah! how many of these little old women have I followed! One among others at the hour when the sinking sun reddens the sky with its scarlet wounds, would sit thoughtfully apart from the crowd on a bench,
To hear one of those concerts, rich in brass, with which soldiers sometimes inundate our gardens and which, in those golden evenings when one's spirit revives, pour heroism into the hearts of citizens.
This old woman, still upright, proud and obedient to rule, greedily drank in this brisk, warlike song; sometimes her eye opened like that of an old eagle; her marble brow seemed made for laurels.

p. 49. I have not forgotten, in the town's neighbourhood, our white house, small but peaceful.

p. 49. The great-hearted servant of whom you were jealous, and who sleeps her sleep under the humble lawn, we should none the less bring her some flowers . . .

p. 50. If, when the log whistles and sings, I should see her quietly seat herself in the armchair; (or) if on a cold blue night in December, I found her nestling in a corner of my bedroom, grave and having come from the depth of her eternal bed to brood with her maternal eyes over the child now grown, what could I reply to that pious soul, seeing tears fall from the hollow lids?

p. 51. –I shall certainly be content for my part to quit a world in which action is not sister to the dream; may I use the sword and perish by the sword! St. Peter denied Jesus . . . he did well!

p. 52. Faithful to his dolorous programme, the author of the *Fleurs du Mal* has been obliged, like a perfect actor, to fashion his mind to suit all sophistries as well as all corruptions.

p. 52. We shall have beds full of light perfumes, divans deep as tombs, and strange flowers on what-nots, opening for us under fairer skies.

As they vie in using up their last fires, our two hearts will burn like two vast torches, reflecting their double lights in our two brains, those twin mirrors.

On an evening of rose and mystic blue, we will exchange a single flash, like a long-drawn sob, laden with adieux; and later an Angel, half-opening the doors, will, faithful and joyous, come to kindle the tarnished mirrors and dead flames.

p. 53. The dreary spectacle of immortal sin.

p. 53. O Death, old captain, it is time! weigh the anchor! This country wearies us, oh Death! Let us set sail! If sky and sea are black as ink, our hearts which are known to you are full of rays!

Pour out thy poison for our comfort! We wish–this fire so burns our brains–to plunge into the deep abyss, Hell or Heaven, what matters it?–the depths of the Unknown to find something *new*!

p. 55. Pascal had his abyss (ever) moving with him. Alas! all is abyss–action, desire, dream, speech! And over the hair (of my skin) which rises upright many a time I feel passing the wind of Fear.

Above, below, on all hands: the bottomless pit, the (empty) strand, silence, frightful yet alluring space . . . On the depth of my nights God with his skilful finger draws a nightmare multiform and uninterrupted.

Sleep I fear as one fears a great hole brimful of vague horror, leading one knows not where. I see nought but the infinite through every window, and my mind, ever haunted by vertigo, envies the insensibility of nothingness.–Oh, never to escape from Numbers and Beings!

p. 56. Of those whose heart says: Blessed be thy scourge, Lord! may suffering, oh Father, be blessed! My soul in thy hands is not a vain plaything, and thy prudence is infinite.

p. 56. Here the author of the *Fleurs du Mal* turns towards the Life eternal. It had to finish like that. Notice that like all new converts he is most rigorous and most fanatical.

BIOGRAPHICAL NOTE

Born on the 9th of April 1821, Charles was the son of François Baudelaire by his second marriage (1819) to Caroline Archimbaut Dufays, an orphan, whose father had been an army officer. Mme Baudelaire knew English and was religious in a feminine way. Her elderly husband was an attractive man who had been tutor in an elegant pre-revolutionary school. With refined tastes and manners he possessed an amateur's gift for the arts. The courage he had shown in helping to effect rescues during the Terror was rewarded by a good administrative post under the Directorate. The year after his death (in 1828), his widow married Major Aupick, an officer of the Légion d'Honneur with a brilliant diplomatic career before him. Promoted lieutenant-colonel, he took his wife and stepson to Lyons, where the boy passed from a preparatory school to the Collège Royal (1833). When they returned to Paris Charles was transferred to the Lycée Louis-le-Grand. His hatred of school did not prevent him from shining as a pupil; he won many prizes including the open competition for Latin verse. Profoundly disturbed by his mother's second marriage, he conceived an ineradicable hatred of his step-father, whose plans for his betterment he resisted in favour of a literary career. During the years 1838-41 Baudelaire haunted the artists' quarter of the Left Bank, reading widely, talking brilliantly, and learning to write, missing none of the excitements and extravagances of Bohemia. Colonel Aupick reacted drastically. He arranged to send the young man on a voyage to India (1841). Charles embarked but would go no further than Mauritius. He returned in the next ship available to celebrate his majority by claiming his inheritance. With this he settled in an expensive flat in the Hôtel Pimodan to enjoy a luxurious existence and to begin serious work. His rapidly increasing debts caused his parents to impose the restraint of a *conseil de famille* and a solicitor, M Ancelle, was appointed to control his allowance. In 1857 *Les Fleurs du Mal*, a collection of a hundred poems, many of which had appeared in reviews, was published and immediately censored; its author was fined 300 francs. When some years later he made a last desperate attempt to raise money for his creditors by giving lectures in Belgium, the venture failed and the ailing poet received a premonition of his end. In 1866, after a seizure, he was taken to a nursing home in Paris where he languished until August 31, 1867. To many of his contemporaries Baudelaire was known as the translator of the tales of Poe. Most of his best prose, including the prose-poems, was collected after his death.

'Discoveries are constantly being made', said M. Jacques Crépet to the writer recently. Three new volumes are to be added to his edition. One will contain Baudelaire's diatribe against the Belgians, which was described as 'épouvantable'. The devoted editor referred to his life's work as having been sustained by 'la passion baudelairienne', caught from his father.

SHORT BIBLIOGRAPHY

The number of books and articles on Baudelaire is already very great; they increase, as do editions of the poems, annually. The following should be available in most British libraries.

I Editions

Baudelaire, C.: *Œuvres Complètes*, édition critique par F. F. Gautier, continuée par Y. G. Le Dantec, Nouvelle Revue Française, Paris, 1918-1937.

Œuvres Complètes, Pléiade edition in 2 vols., 1918.

Œuvres Complètes, Conard, Paris, 1922-1939. Standard edition by the Baudelairian specialist, J. Crépet.

Les Fleurs du Mal, vol. I. of complete works (1868-70), with important preface by Théophile Gautier.

Les Fleurs du Mal, José Corti, Paris, 1942. Edited by J. Crépet and G. Blin. Most recent scholarly edition.

Les Fleurs du Mal, Blackwell, Oxford, 1943. Edited by Enid Starkie. Most convenient edition.

Correspondance Générale, Conard, Paris, 1947.

Journaux Intimes, José Corti, Paris, 1949. Critical edition by J. Crépet and G. Blin.

II Works of Reference

Blin, G.: *Baudelaire*, Paris, 1939. Important study of the poet's thought.

Clapton, G. T.: *Baudelaire et De Quincey*, Paris, 1931. Succinct, a model of its kind.

Chérix, R. B.: *Commentaire des 'Fleurs du Mal'*, Geneva, 1949. Interesting.

Crépet, E.-J.: *Baudelaire*, Paris, 1907. The basic biography.

Ferran, A.: *L'Esthétique de Baudelaire*, Paris, 1933. The most comprehensive study.

Fondane, B.: *Baudelaire et l'Expérience du Gouffre*, Paris, 1947. Interesting but unrevised.

Massin, J.: *Baudelaire: Entre Dieu et Satan*, Paris, 1945. The religious problem.

Parmée, D.: *Selected Critical Essays of Baudelaire*, with introduction, Cambridge, 1949.

Peyre, H.: *Connaissance de Baudelaire*, Paris, 1951. Invaluable for reference and bibliography.

Pommier, J.: *La Mystique de Baudelaire*, Paris, 1932.

Dans les Chemins de Baudelaire, Paris, 1945. Important for the background.

Porché, F.: *La Vie Douloureuse de Baudelaire*, Paris, 1925.

Quennell, P.: *Baudelaire and the Symbolists*, London, 1929.

Rhodes, S. A.: *The Cult of Beauty in Baudelaire*, London, 1929.

Sartre, J. P.: *Baudelaire*, précédé d'une notice de M. Leuris, Paris, 1947. English translation by Martin Turnell, London, 1949.

Starkie, E.: *Baudelaire*, London, 1933.

III

Among shorter studies or articles the following are recommended:

Bourget, P.: 'Baudelaire' in *Essais de Psychologie contemporaine*, Paris, 1899.

Du Bos, C.: Introduction to *Baudelaire: Mon Coeur mis à Nu*, Paris, 1930.

'Baudelaire' *Approximations*, vol. 4. Important for the poet's psychology.

Eliot, T. S.: 'Baudelaire'. Introduction to *Journaux Intimes*, translated by Christopher Isherwood (Blackamore Press). Collected in *Selected Essays*, second edition, London, 1934. Unequalled in English: perceives the height and depth of the subject and the power of visionary realism.

'Baudelaire and our Time' in *Essays Ancient and Modern*, London, 1936. Castigates A. Symons' translation and his view of B. as 'hermit of the Brothel'.

Murry, J. M.: 'Baudelaire' in *Countries of the Mind*, London, 1922. Good on aspects of the art and imagery.

Valéry, P.: *Situation de Baudelaire*. Introduction to *Les Fleurs du Mal*, Paris, 1930. Collected in *Variété II*. Interesting.